A wonderfully languorous piece of time travel back to the so-called Golden Age of cricket' *Guardian*

DUNCAN HAMILTON is a journalist who has won three William Hill Sports Book of the Year prizes. He has been nominated on a further four occasions. He has also claimed two British Sports Book awards and is the first writer to have won the Wisden Cricket Book of the Year three times. His biography of the Chariots of Fire runner Eric Liddell, *For the Glory*, was a *New York Times* bestseller.

Other cricket books by Duncan Hamilton

Harold Larwood: The Biography

A Last English Summer

The Kings of Summer

A Clear Blue Sky (with Jonny Bairstow)

Wisden on Yorkshire (ed.)

Sweet Summers: The Cricket Writing of J. M. Kilburn

The Great Romantic: Cricket and the Golden Age of Neville Cardus

ONE LONG AND BEAUTIFUL SUMMER

A short elegy for red-ball cricket

Duncan Hamilton

riverrun

First published in Great Britain in 2020
This paperback edition published in 2021 by

riverrun

An imprint of

Quercus Editions Ltd
Carmelite House
50 Victoria Embankment
London EC4Y 0DZ

An Hachette UK company
Copyright © 2020 Duncan Hamilton

A CIP catalogue record for this book is available
from the British Library

Paperback 978 1 52940 839 3
eBook 978 1 52940 838 6

10 9 8 7 6 5 4 3 2 1

Typeset by CC Book Production
Printed and bound in Great Britain by Clays Ltd, Elcograf S.p.A.

Papers used by Quercus Editions Ltd are from well-managed forests
and other responsible sources.

To Peter Wynne-Thomas,
the Sage of Trent Bridge

Contents

Introduction to the Paperback Edition

The photographer Henri Cartier-Bresson said he tried to capture with his camera 'the decisive moment' and hold it 'immobile'.

This was the first and most straightforward objective of *One Long and Beautiful Summer*: to preserve both a place and the people in it (cricketers and spectators alike) on the day that I observed them. The second objective, implicit in the title, was to look back at all the cricket I'd watched for a half century and also to look forward at what might or might not await the game in the near future. I went into 2019 with a premonitory sense of loss, waiting for The Hundred to swing into the following season, like a wrecking ball, and start the process of demolishing to dust some of the things I hold dear.

You know what happened next.

History really is just one damned thing after another, which is why we don't always recognise an event as being truly historic while we're living through it. But we did in 2020, the year when nothing seemed unimaginable.

Spring was crouching in the grass when 'Covid-19' and 'social distancing' and 'face masks' and 'furlough' slipped into our life and our language. I didn't think about cricket much until the shock had worn off and I finally, if reluctantly, accepted the parameters of the 'new normal' and had adapted to them, more or less.

In that period when I had time on my hands but absolutely nowhere to go, and it looked as though no cricket would be played at all, I spent a lot of hours staring at the colourful fixture wallchart published annually by *The Cricketer*. As a collector and a near obsessive hoarder of ephemera, I was always going to save it – a little keepsake of the summer that never was – but the wallchart served a purpose beyond that of quirky souvenir.

The Championship games, perhaps deliberately, appear on it like blocks of gradated sky: a slightly diluted Winsor Blue for Division One and vivid Cerulean for Division Two. It was sad and yet paradoxically consoling to look at them and know where I would have been if the fixture list had been fulfilled according to plan. I thought about the journeys I would have taken. I saw myself in the following places. Sitting between the tea bar and the Festival diner at Scarborough. Walking through the Dixon Memorial Gates at Trent Bridge. Admiring the white tents and perhaps a line of bunting at Guildford or at Merchant Taylor's School. Catching the train from Liverpool Street, leaving the noise of London behind and arriving in Chelmsford to watch the Champions, Essex.

Publication of *One Long and Beautiful Summer* was still some way off then. I began to fret that the season I'd seen and strived to celebrate in print already seemed irrelevant and could only become more pointless as the weeks passed.

In fact, exactly the opposite occurred.

First the absence of the game – and then the fact the ordinary fan couldn't be there to watch the matches that were played – made 2019 more relevant than it otherwise would have been. We appreciated cricket more because we felt the loss of it so keenly; indeed, the previous summer appeared almost prelapsarian.

As the blank days piled up, becoming months, and the summer got older, it occurred to me how damned lucky I'd been to spend 2019 chasing the sun in so many lovely spots, such as Hove and Taunton, York and North Nottinghamshire. Even following my local village club was a blessing.

As I write this, I have no clue – and nor does anyone else – about how much cricket we might get in 2021 or whether we'll be able to sit beside a friend or a complete stranger and grumble about the weather while drinking our tea.

This may be crassly optimistic, but I've already made tentative plans in anticipation that all (or nearly all) will be well, possibly by the second half of the season. My bag, so to speak, is already half-packed. A little bit of me is even missing snooty Lord's – and that's a sentiment I never expected to express.

When I do stroll into a ground again, wherever it is, I know what I'll feel will be close to reverence.

Duncan Hamilton, Wharfedale, February, 2021

Mason Crane, about to display the craft
that both tempts and threatens

A Leg-spinner from the Scoreboard End

Stealing the Grace Gates. The Holbein King. A sort of wicketkeeper–batsman. An addict's craving for the game. The newspaperman and his hut. Geoffrey Boycott's memory. A delivery that dripped like honey.

The ground occupies an unlikely dot on the map. It is one of those inconspicuous, middle-of-nowhere places that you barely notice and would normally pass through in a hurry on the way to somewhere else. Search for it and you might even suppose you're lost, or are heading completely in the wrong direction, until a sign tells you to turn off the A60. I saw first the pointy tip of a marquee, pegged out for the occasion. The rest of the ground was camouflaged by the shallow rise of lush fields, tall, plump trees and high hedges.

It was the second Sunday in June. Long stretches of the roadside verges were crammed with poppies, glowingly iridescent, cornflowers and short, fat clumps of cowslips.

Welbeck Colliery Cricket Club is in Sookholme, which isn't quite a hamlet but only just qualifies as a village. I confess that I had never heard of it before. There is a squat Norman chapel, named after St Augustine, a scattering of red-roofed homes and a tropical-fish emporium. In the middle distance – crowning the ridge of a wide, steepish hill – sits a wood, which is dense and dark green. Beyond the wood is that wide roll of countryside that will always belong to two diverse heroes of the county: D. H. Lawrence, who planted much of his fiction in it, and Harold Larwood, who climbed out of a pit and learned how to bowl fast on scrubby pitches, his phenomenal pace turning him into a cricketing immortal.

No smaller place had ever staged a County Championship match. Nottinghamshire had decamped here from Trent Bridge as a consequence of the World Cup, the competition temporarily exiling them from home. That was a blessing. The game, against Hampshire, got framed within a landscape so very pastoral and so very English at the root. I looked across the ground and saw what everyone – fan and non-fan alike – imagines is the ideal scene for cricket; the kind, in fact, that the wing-collared Victorian Hugh de Sélincourt would have celebrated in his novel, *The Cricket Match*.

There was a low brick pavilion with a balcony and a

pediment. There were white tents, the most sumptuous cake stall imaginable tucked into one of them. There was a boundary rope, thick enough to tie up a ship in port. There was a scoreboard with a cupola, a pale-faced clock set handsomely into it. There was row-upon-row of tip-up seats. And, as these began to fill, the prime views claimed in a dash, like the last prize in a game of musical chairs, picnic baskets and rugs were laid down, sandwich boxes got snapped open and tea was poured from huge flasks. I saw spectators, waiting for the eleven o'clock start, turn to the sports sections of newspapers or scrutinise the latest *Playfair*, the spine already well cracked.

Electricity pylons dominated the skyline, stretching from east to west as though marching towards the horizon in long strides. Far from despoiling the view, they somehow added a peculiar charm to it. The pylons are an identifying feature at Sookholme in the same way that the gasometer is at The Oval. One of the sight screens, not much more than a gargantuan bed sheet, was a dingy grey, as if it had been accidentally shoved into the washing machine with a pair of black socks. That didn't matter either.

If coloured bunting had been strung between the tents, and if a uniformed brass band had played in that part of the field where the covers stood, the whole thing would have resembled a particularly jolly country-house fete. I even imagined W. G. Grace emerging in the bulbous flesh from the acres of wheat close by, his Select XI filing out behind him at first light in the cricketing equivalent of *Field of Dreams*. There would be Wilfred Rhodes and F. S. Jackson, perhaps, and Spofforth, the brimstone Demon of Australia, tossing a shiny ball from hand to hand as casually as he would an apple. And, no doubt, emerging from the opposite corner would be Jack Hobbs with his immaculately clean brown bat. He'd be about to open once more with Herbert Sutcliffe, his shirt cuffs folded to the elbow and his hair brilliantined to a fabulous sheen. Of course, Larwood would be there too, the obvious pick, and he'd be standing next to his pal, the barrel-chested Bill Voce, the deadly double act of Bodyline reunited. As for their old Notts captain, the benignly incorrigible Arthur Carr . . . well, I suspect he'd have already got the beers in and would be on his second gin and tonic chaser.

Sookholme is that sort of spot. It is a good place to bring your thoughts and also to daydream a little.

We have all gazed out of the window of a train, or passed a patch of good-looking fields in the countryside, and had a whimsical thought: this would make a cricket pitch. We have gone as far as to sketch out a plan – albeit only in our minds – as though we were Thomas Lord. We have known instinctively where the entrance would be. Where the square would be cut. Where the pavilion ought to stand and how it would look. We have worked out where the afternoon and early evening sun would slant across the land, the shadows cast month by month telling us as reliably as a timepiece how much of the summer was left.

I often build the ideal ground this way, mapping it out architecturally, bit by lovely bit. It would be a combination of Trent Bridge, Taunton, Scarborough and Canterbury. From Trent Bridge, I would take the stately Victorian pavilion with its balustrades, white woodwork and hanging baskets, each a shot of effulgent colour. I would bottle the atmosphere from there too: grand but intimate and never aloof or unfriendly. From Taunton, I would filch the church of St James with its noble 116-foot tower, crocketed finials and pieced parapets. From Scarborough, where the gulls wheel in off the North Sea, I would borrow both the Popular Bank, the wooden benches that turn the field into a shallow bowl and a row or two of high terraced housing, where sometimes you glimpse pegged-out washing in the back yard. From Canterbury, I would uproot the lime and dig a hole for it at cow corner. The tree would be as it once was: tall and broad, the lower branches a dark umbrella.

Lord's is always far too snooty for me, a high church I prefer not to worship in. I feel I ought to wear a suit, a tie and a pair of dress shoes even to sit in the upper tier of the Compton Stand. But I would filch a few 'odds and ends', gleaned from there, for ornamental purposes. I have a fondness for the Grace Gates and the old Father Time weathervane. I would loot some of the MCC's collection of art as well, particularly

Albert Chevallier Tayler's masterpiece, *Kent versus Lancashire at Canterbury in 1906*, which captures the genteel splendour of Edwardian England, and Brendan Kelly's portrait of Viv Richards. In a thin, unpretentious frame, almost seven-feet square, you get nothing but Richards's magnificent head and his hefty shoulders. He is dressed in civvies rather than whites. The face and the expression on it convey instantly – even to those only partly acquainted with the game – everything that distinguished Richards as the Superman of batting. That power. That composure and phlegmatic command. That regal bearing and gum-chewing swagger. There are painters who, even after eyeballing their sitter from six feet and for months on end, can't find the soul beneath the skin and so never discover the intricate, myriad pieces that make up a man. Kelly's canvas *is* Richards absolutely; he's as royal in oil as a Holbein king.

Of course, there'd be a second-hand book stall on my perfect ground (exactly like the one you'll find during the Cheltenham Festival) and the shelves would be stocked with those rare titles you'd always been searching for. And there would be striped deckchairs (as at Hove). And there would be a printer's shop cranking out scorecards, the smell of ink pungently strong. And dogs would be encouraged to loll about on the boundary edge. And afternoon tea would arrive in big brown pots (for the sound of boiling water, poured from the spout, is just *so* comforting). And at lunch you would be allowed on to the outfield to play a miniature game with a bat and tennis ball. From a respectful distance you would be able to watch the ground staff sweep dust from the pitch or fill in and smooth flat the bowler's footmarks with one of those long-handled, wooden contraptions that looks fierce enough to kill someone with a single blow.

I thought of all this at Sookholme, mightily envious that someone had gone further than just imagining the ground he wanted. It is the work of one man. I gazed around and saw a small monument to his generosity.

John Fretwell, a local entrepreneur, bought 19 acres of farmland, dug them over, put in drainage and smoothed and seeded the clay soil. What is more, he didn't keep it solely for himself afterwards, which would have been a temptation for the rest of us. He gifted the ground instead to his local club, where decades before he had been 'a sort of wicketkeeper–batsman'. The community mattered to him because he and generations of Fretwells had grown up in it. The ground cost him £3 million. It was completed in 2006. The money earned to achieve this act of philanthropy came from sweat and guts and ingenuity rather than a lottery winner's luck.

To describe Fretwell as self-made is to undersell the extraordinariness of his story and the zeal behind it. This began quietly about half a century ago. He was a barber, who cut hair for a few bob, worked until 11 p.m. two nights a week and asked his customers: 'Anything for the weekend, sir?' When a salesman, who usually sold shampoo, offered him a few watches at a discount price, Fretwell took a chance on them. He had £34, the equivalent of £190 today. That sum constituted his life savings. He bought 17 watches at £2 each. Within four days, he had sold the lot from a suitcase at a profit of almost £13. He immediately replenished his stock, getting rid of another 84. You do the maths. So it went on. What followed was one success after another, the sideline becoming a flourishing business. When Fretwell, who is 70 now, sold his wholesale firm, shortly after the turn of this century, he had a staff of 650, an office in China and dealt in more than 1,000 products. Sookholme has staged A-list games before; Fretwell took tickets at the gate and only the regulars, who recognised him, were aware of the incongruity of that sight.

If you have ever been to Wormsley, you will know what John Paul Getty created there. If you haven't, then you should go to the next fixture. Wormsley, which aspires to absolute perfection and seldom falls short of it, is not only Getty's abundant thank you to a game with which he belatedly became completely besotted, even taking over the company that owned *Wisden*. It also demonstrates his swooning adoration for England – and, most obviously, the way he viewed the country and what attracted him to it. Wormsley, hidden in the Chilterns, is about a bygone England of the sort Evelyn Waugh would have recognised and approved of. Every bit of Wormsley evokes warm beer and old, heavy pennies in your pocket. There are thatched roofs, a red telephone box, tall flagpoles and a mock Tudor pavilion. The grass looks as though a battalion of obsessively fastidious gardeners clip it with nail scissors. The countryside around the ground appears to sweep softly into infinity. After a while, seduced by that prospect, you almost stop believing that urban sprawl and some dirty city are lying over the next hill; it just doesn't seem possible. When I first went there, I sat on the boundary and a red kite swooped over my head, so low that I saw the distinct markings on the underside of its huge wings.

The ground in Sookholme is humbler and earthier. Less than four miles away lies what is left of a mine that, for nearly a century, guaranteed employment to 1,400 men in its roaring heyday and to over 400 before the last tubs of coal got hauled out of the shaft at the beginning of the decade. As much as I love it, and always want to return, Wormsley is a decorative ground, primarily for decorative cricket, where the result isn't necessarily as important as the white-wine-and-cheese sociability of the day and the enjoyment you draw from the views. But, at Sookholme, I appreciated all over again why the County Championship has been such an integral slice of my life for almost 50 years; why, indeed, every season I go back to it eagerly as an entertainment, as a solace and for convalescence sometimes and as a pleasure always – even on days that are fridge-cold or spotted with rain, which makes attendance seem like martyrdom, or when the scoring and the over rate progress at a funereal pace and a game is so sparsely attended that I could shake hands with everyone there in less than a quarter of an hour.

Alan Ross wrote that occasionally a match bored and exasperated him. He would head for home but want to know what was happening as soon as he left the ground. It typified what Ross called his 'addict's craving' for cricket which 'only the extinction of it or myself can cure'.

I know – as many others will too – precisely what he meant.

There is an article by John Arlott that I re-read at least once a season. It curiously isn't about a player, a match or even one of the great characters of the game. Arlott writes about a newspaper seller named Arthur Smith, who worked from a wooden hut at Headingley and also at Yorkshire's out grounds. The piece begins when Arlott finds 'Smithy' wearing a shirt 'open at the neck', his white coat 'catching the breeze', his hair 'swept back to the neck-line as sharp as a razor'. Something different about him startles Arlott immediately. Smithy sports a suntan that 'would have turned a Riviera life-saver green with envy', he says. Arlott learns his friend has spent the winter in Australia. He sold his van and the tools of his part-time plumbing trade, raising £100 for his passage. Arriving in Perth with a small trunk, an overnight case and £15 in his wallet, he embarked on a working holiday throughout the Ashes series. On the second day of the Adelaide Test, he broke a personal best: he sold 1,224 newspapers. To save money, Smithy slept in a bus shelter and twice bedded down on a park bench. He gave up alcohol and cigarettes for the duration of the tour too. After buying gifts for his patient family, he returned home with £7, which was presented to Mrs Smith. I relish the piece so much, not only because Smithy, endearing and brilliantly eccentric, is so affectionately drawn, but also because his adventures remind me that newspapers were once so popular and so full of cricket that people actually thought it was worth buying them.

I read Arlott's description of him again after the match at Sookholme was over. Our national newspapers have practically given up on the County Championship unless something stupendous or quirky occurs in a game. The days are regretfully long gone when, as Peter Roebuck highlighted in his diary *It Never Rains,* the players sought out the *Daily Telegraph* with a religious fervour because 'it reports on every game and so by studying it, every cricketer can follow the fortunes of every other player in his enclosed world'. The *Telegraph*, once upon a time the Bible of county coverage, devoted only eighty-nine words to Nottinghamshire against Hampshire. *The Times* condensed their report into a dozen fewer.

The facts of an undramatic match were these: Notts, already marooned at the bottom of the table, were in awful trouble from the third ball of the first over and made only a semi-fist of fighting back afterwards. The previous week, against Warwickshire, they had wilted embarrassingly to 97 all out. The top order malfunctioned miserably again at Sookholme; so much so that the most experienced of them looked as though it was their first day on the job. Even one of my favourite players, Samit Patel, who does everything with a heroic optimism, was subdued and out of sorts. He sweated for 69 balls, making 24. It was the second-highest score of the innings. His only support came from Steve Mullaney; he spent nearly three hours gallantly grinding out 45 before, like a good captain, becoming the last man to fall.

A big, quick bowler looks bigger still on a small field. Kyle Abbott, who played 11 Tests for South Africa, is 6 foot 3 inches tall. His legs are long – you half-expected him to start his run in inside the hospitality tent – but his arms look longer still. It was as if, halfway to the stumps, he had somehow extended them by another foot. Abbott bullied the batsmen, the bounce and movement he generated off the pitch bringing him six for 37. Notts worked hard to eke out only 167, doing so painfully, because elbow grease can only take you so far. Hampshire's reply, 93 for two at the close, was all we and Sookholme got. Not another ball was bowled. As it so often did during that blighted month – when bands of low pressure drifted across from the Atlantic every week – the rain came and refused to go, washing the rest of the match away.

While far too brief a treat, the game was memorable for one reason. The charm of the Championship was soaked right through it. Like all the finest out-grounds – Radlett, Basingstoke and Arundel, for instance – you could feel every breath the match took. The ball might fly your way and then you would know what it was like to run your fingers over the bony ridge of the seam. A boundary fielder – in this case, Hampshire's Rilee Rossouw – would tell you about the state of the pitch. The coaches, the twelfth man and those who had already batted, or were waiting to bat lower down the order, would saunter about, also talking amiably of what had already happened or could happen later on. The high stands and cavernous splendour of a Test venue, such as The Oval or the Ageas Bowl, are imposing only when full to burst. When three quarters empty or half closed-off, and the echo of someone politely coughing disturbs the air, you feel so distant and semi-detached from what is going on that you could be looking at it through the wrong end of an observatory telescope. At Sookholme, where everything is up close and personal, you are on top of the play and almost become a participant in it. The Championship, which revels in that sort of mood, needs to be fought out on fields like that one and also against a sublimely beautiful backdrop. Concrete and steel and swathes of unoccupied seats do it no favours.

We witnessed a day of manual labour, rather than magnificent stroke play, but Sookholme confirmed that J. M. Kilburn was right. It was Kilburn, correspondent of the *Yorkshire Post*, who pointed out that 'something' worthwhile, 'something' striking, emerges from every match – even from those in which, for hours, nothing much happens in a kind of *Waiting for Godot* way. You require the patience of a birdwatcher until the eye finally opens and shuts on what you have been waiting for, preserving it like a photograph. It doesn't have to be a monumental moment either. A catch taken nimbly. A sprawling stop in which the fielder's flannels are stained with grass. A shot that goes off the bat with a crack.

In one respect, the most experienced cricket-watchers are like the most experienced cricketers. They have in common a fabulously capacious memory and the capacity for astonishing feats of recall. Wish-fulfilment, as well as a need to please, means the traveller is always susceptible to the minor, very human flaw of wanting to tell you a tad more than he actually saw. You have to make allowances for that. I am, nonetheless, never surprised when someone who has either played in a game or simply seen it can recount verbatim, as though the action is spooling right in front of them, a single ball or an entire over or even every stitch and pleat and tuck of a match. Geoffrey Boycott does this effortlessly, as if everything he is remembering occurred only ten minutes ago. You get from him the score, the look of the field, the weather and even the contents of someone's lunch tin. One of the reasons we belt out song lyrics, but often stumble whenever we try to recite poetry accurately, is the emotional trigger a few chords of music set off. Those chords lead us towards the words. Cricket has that same emotional trigger. We remember what happened so vividly because we solidly connect peripheral events – the appearance of the ground, the statistics of the match and the emotions we experienced – to the main one, spotlighting the thing in near-neon.

I can still see a ball from Andy Roberts bowled more than

40 years ago. Or, more to the point, I can see the consequence of it: one of Tony Greig's stumps ripped out and airborne, the defensive prod made a microsecond too late to prevent such ignominy. I see Alan Knott, a boyhood hero, airborne too, his blood-red gloves taking a wayward leg-side delivery from John Snow. The energetic leap and the catch, achieved horizontally, made Knott look as though he had been abruptly hoisted upwards and then suddenly tugged sideways on some invisible zip wire. And I see Roberts again, this time stationed on the boundary, beneath a steepling catch that David Steele has hooked towards him with an uncharacteristic rashness.

Like anyone else, I can reach out and pull down a thousand and one memories like that. The mention of a name or the return to a specific place are sufficient to start that process. In early April, I travelled to Trent Bridge because it seemed so apt. Notts, the team I followed while growing up, were facing Yorkshire, my local team now. Joe Root was playing, pitted against the bowling of Stuart Broad. It is always important to go *somewhere* on the season's opening day, which for the true devotee has the same thrill as a childhood Christmas morning. Trent Bridge was finely dressed for the occasion, the scent of fresh paint detectable, but the ground stood half in sun and half in shadow, the clouds reluctant to shift. We got a little brightness and a little attritional gloom.

Not long after lunch, Notts's Chris Nash drove an over-pitched delivery from Matthew Waite so gracefully through extra cover and towards the scoreboard that it startled even the drowsiest spectator awake. It was gorgeous. Nash held his pose for a while – bat high, left elbow bent, left foot in perfect alignment with the direction of the ball as it fizzed along the floor. The next delivery, slightly wide, was begging to be cut. Nash took a swish at it. His effort was ugly and mistimed. He got a razory bottom edge. The ball dropped in front of the slips and streaked away, stopping only when it thumped softly against the pavilion's advertising boards. The first shot evoked Woolley or Hammond or Gower. The second made Nash look like a tail-ender who hardly knew which end of the bat to hold. Such is cricket. Those few minutes are how my memory chooses to remember the whole of that match.

What, for me, defined the game at Sookholme wasn't dramatic either. I guess it was soon forgotten by everyone else.

In the morning there had been a sharp shower, lasting less than half an hour, which forced the players off for lunch prematurely. A slight breeze then arrived and carried away the worst of the cloud, leaving only a few fluffy rags of it behind. It became surprisingly hot. Ideally, you needed the broad brim of one of those Van Gogh straw hats for protection against the sun.

Hampshire had been plugging away with pace, chiefly because of Abbott's successes, which it seemed ridiculous to interrupt. But just after quarter past four, as tea approached, the ball was handed to the leg-spinner Mason Crane. Still only

22, slight and blondish, Crane arrived as a welcome respite from the grunt of seam. You greeted him like the surprise visitor you most wanted to find at your front door.

J. B. Priestley wrote a book called *Delight*, his Grand Tour of the ordinary and everyday things that both satisfied and inspired him. Smoking in a hot bath. Buying a new box of matches. The smell of breakfast bacon. The paintings of Vermeer. Reading detective stories in bed. Watching a ship sail out of port. You read it and realise that you know a man best by the sort of Utopia in which he desires to live. My Utopia – on a cricket field at least – is watching a leg-spinner.

There are moments at a match for me – these usually occur in high summer and during late afternoon or early evening – when I look around and experience a blissful contentment. At the arch of the sky. At the slow drop of the sun. At the stripy cut of the grass. I get so absorbed in the scene that I entirely forget the rest of the world and what is going on in it. Nothing else is of *any* consequence. That feeling is so wonderfully therapeutic; I am reluctant to snap out of it.

It happened again watching Crane.

Even at such a tender age, the full arc of his career still forming, he has already experienced the impostors of triumph and disaster and treated them with as much equanimity as he can muster. The highs have been an Ashes series in Australia and a Cup final win at Lord's. The lows, pitch black, have been injuries, including two back fractures. Until this season began, Crane hadn't played anywhere for nine months, knowing only too well the inside of a gym and the grind of practising in the nets until his spinning fingers were sore.

He began bowling with his back to the scoreboard. I watched his first two overs while standing at the opposite end with a friend. Crane bounced towards the crease, his arms a small whirl of activity during a seven-stride run. He gave the odd ball a lot of air. On the one hand, he invited the batsman to drive very straight to the short boundary. On the other, he nagged him about the danger of doing exactly that.

I saw his third and last over from a seat at wide mid-off. One delivery, from close to the stumps, was teasingly floated. The next, faster and flatter, was arrowed in a little wider. As Crane wheeled away, I thought about watching Shane Warne bowl for Hampshire a decade before. Through binoculars I had tried as best I could to follow the sharp turn or swift flick of his wrist, attempting to predict what variation of speed and flight awaited whoever was facing him. Once, I recall, Warne bowled a ball so slowly and gave it so much loop that following the drop of it was like watching honey drip from a twisting spoon. And because I thought about Warne, who only showed his cards one at a time, I also began to think about Abdul Qadir, his wrong 'un an immense and delightful puzzle that demanded to be solved in less than a second, and also Intikhab Alam, who would lick his fingers at the top of his run, like a bank teller about to count a wad of ten-pound notes. I thought, too, about Robin Hobbs, the sort of bowler who needed no advice about the virtues of perseverance. I saw him bowl while wrapped in two long-sleeved cable-knit sweaters, the day so bitter that he had to blow on to his fingers between deliveries to grip the ball.

Though tempting and threatening, Crane didn't take a wicket. He didn't bowl a maiden. I didn't care. The sky was richly blue. The faintest shimmer of a heat haze appeared across the distant hills. A leg-spinner was bowling, displaying his craft. There was some polite applause and then the crowd stirred at the end of the over, murmuring to itself. Crane took his cap from the umpire, tugged down the peak and walked into the outfield. The civilised beauty of the County Championship was encapsulated for me in every gesture, presented like a gift. On that lovely Sunday afternoon, I got lost in the moment and I thought also of others like it.

I saw my first Championship match in 1970. Only 20 years before, Donald Bradman had published *Farewell to Cricket*. The last ball of the Bodyline series had been bowled a mere 17 years before that. Still alive then were old men of Victorian stock, 'grey and full of sleep', who had an end-of-the-century formality about them. They were capable not only of remembering Victoria in her widow's weeds, but also Victor Trumper in full flow. A goodly number of them claimed to have seen Grace bat and were anxious to let you know about it. Their past and W. G.'s own were antique to me, like a sepia print or an aspidistra in a brass pot, and the span of Time being revisited seemed to have occurred so long ago that Herodotus could have written the history of it. Now, especially to the generation raised on the white-ball game, I surely sound like them, a croaky and whiskery veteran nostalgically summoning ghosts. Maybe that's who I am and also what I do; but it seems poignant, and even very necessary to be doing it at this hour.

Modernity is all the rage and it comes at you at such a fast lick. You're in the day after tomorrow almost before you realise yesterday has gone. Amid the carnival hurly-burly, the slow trot of the Championship can seem as anachronistic as a coal fire or the sight of a shire horse pulling a plough. But for those of us who regard winter as a punishment, and spring and summer as our reward for coming through it, that fact constitutes part of the competition's distinctive charm.

I like the nuanced complexity of the Championship. I like the contemplative discipline required to watch it. I like the dramatic flow of a match, changing completely sometimes in only a session, an hour or in ten mad minutes when three wickets are taken. I like those final mornings when any result is possible. I even like the sort of game that ought to have been declared a draw on the third afternoon. Aside, quite obviously, from being there when some bowler runs through batting like a lance, or some batsman thrashes the bowling to pulp, I like the stonewaller who can defend against the clock and in such unfavourable conditions that what ought to be boring actually becomes fascinating. White-ball cricket has winnowed the species to near extinction – no Bailey and Tavaré types today – so coming across a survivor is like finding a nightjar resting on a branch in your back garden.

I like packing for a match too: pen and notebook, a news-paper, flat cap, scarf, suntan lotion, radio, binoculars. I like getting there so early that a stillness is in the air. I like wandering around the ground, assessing the play from every compass point. I like to follow the scores from elsewhere. The Championship is never quite in fashion. I suppose I like that fact too; the competition is a 'secret' I and fellow lovers of it can keep more or less to ourselves.

There is one more thing.

Look hard enough and the character of the Championship reflects and embodies who we are: the polite decency and the diversity of the country; the patience, forbearance and tolerance we possess; the quirks and whimsical rituals performed in our daily lives; an obsession with – and stoic acceptance of – the weather; our pride in our scenery, which is a feast for the eye, and our appreciation of our architectural heritage; our reverence for history and tradition; our kindness towards strangers (you're never short of chatty company at a cricket match); and our fast determination, come what may, to carry on and enjoy ourselves.

But the game I adore is about to experience a paradigm shift. It may never be quite the same again. That's why I left Sookholme with a curious sense of homesickness for a place I was already in.

The Oval, 1938: Len Hutton, described by Edmund Blunden as
that 'marvellous boy', during his world record 364 against Australia.

CHAPTER ONE

Something That Once Seemed His For Ever

A copy of Wisden *on a winter's afternoon. The ECB and the circus. The County Championship slowly disappears.*
The forgotten book. Air strokes in front of the bedroom mirror.

It began like this.

It was bleak mid-January, one of those short and forlornly grey days that depress you because there is never enough strong light to fill them. The darkness made everything a little claustrophobic. By late afternoon, the shadows growing thicker, it felt like being in a room with contracting walls. Spring seemed impossibly far off then. The antidote for that wintery gloom is a two-part ritual I perform every year at about the same time. I look at the County Championship fixtures; I order *Wisden* with some ceremony, another way of drawing the new season a bit closer.

To travel anywhere in this country is nearly always a fuss and regularly a frustration. Our roads are either clogged with traffic or being dug up. Our railways run on a clock contrary to everyone else's, as though Greenwich Mean Time is negotiable once you set foot in a station. As for our buses . . . well, if you're fortunate enough to find a stop, the bus is usually so slow and creeps along such a labyrinthine route that it is frequently quicker to walk. But in the beginning, thinking of the new season, I never find any of that off-putting because the swell of anticipation takes over. The point of departure and of arrival are lovely to contemplate; I don't spoil the moment with thoughts about the difficulties that are sure to occur in between. So in my mind, I am always travelling hopefully and the sun is yellow-bright and very full, as though a child has drawn it with a crayon.

I got out the fixtures, spreading them across the table like a map. Of course, I would go to Trent Bridge and sit, where I have always done, as close as possible to the spot where George Parr's tree once stood, the high branches protecting Bridgford Road from being peppered with his sixes during the nineteenth century. I would go to Scarborough, where the waves of the North Sea have worn the town's wide bays into smooth, sandy curves. I would go to Hove and walk along the pier and the prom at Brighton. I would go to Lord's for my annual squabble with a white-coated steward about where it is and is not permissible to sit in practically deserted stands (visiting Lord's is compulsory, but I am reconciled to the fact that I will always be a trespasser there, never quite able to fit in or feel comfortably at home). There were other intriguing possibilities, each worth packing a suitcase for: Kent at Beckenham; Yorkshire at York. Lancashire among the blue-purple hills of Sedburgh; Glamorgan and Hampshire at two different Newports, a distance of 151 miles separating Spytty Park in south Wales and the Isle of Wight. There were a scattering of club grounds and villages where I thought about going too, the standard of the game less significant than the splendour of the setting and the effect it has on you: a well-tended ground, flanked by a river or fringed by heavy trees, a church spire rising over long leg and a pub's high brick chimney poking above deep extra cover.

I scribbled copious pencilled notes, the lines running across one another and stretching to the far corners of the paper. Listing destinations beside dates, I discovered that I had frequently sent myself to two places at once; and also that sometimes these places were motorways apart from one another. I rubbed things out and then put them back in again, deciding eventually not to be tied to a calendar even of my own making. Wherever I went would be determined on a whim or because circumstance took me there.

This all felt much more urgent than it ever had done in the past. How could it not? Everything has a last time, and I knew those of us devoted to the Championship must wring out, drop by drop, what is left of it during cricket's final summer before the revolution.

The wall chart produced by *The Cricketer* for the 2019 season required more colours (21 of them) to represent the different forms of the game than you'll find in a Matisse exhibition. Adding The Hundred could necessitate asking Winsor & Newton to mix a completely new one for the occasion.

Ever since Twenty20 was born and took infant steps in the early noughties, the gravitational pull of the game has been tilting, incrementally at first and then at a disturbingly rapid clip, from the red ball to the white. Modern sport barely exists, and certainly can't flourish, unless it is screened live and regularly. Satellite TV is solely about the live action it provides. You can't gather in subscribers – and you definitely can't retain them – by offering recorded highlights of what happened last night or yesterday afternoon. Only *the now* counts. Sky Sports soon came to adore Twenty20 because all the entertainment and punchy drama could be crammed into three hours or thereabouts. You don't have the bother of waiting an entire day, as you do in a Test or in the Championship, for a match to unfold gradually, like the petals of a flower. Twenty20 games, liberally sprinkled about, also conveniently fill entire weeks of programming.

But even Twenty20 is too long for some people who, impatient and restless, want something shorter still and boiled down to the bones. That mutation is The Hundred, which always strikes me as a good title for a pulp novel of derring-do with a particularly gaudy cover. More bells-and-whistle gimmicks will be squeezed into far fewer deliveries. More inappropriately ridiculous names and new, garish kit will attach themselves to city-based franchises. The Roses Match will be between Manchester Originals and Northern Superchargers rather than Lancashire and Yorkshire. Had he not been cremated, Neville Cardus would be rising from his grave . . .

The English Cricket Board's strategy is to bastardise aspects of the game specifically to appeal to people who don't like cricket. The people who do like it, and those of us who are particularly fond of the Championship, seem to be immaterial to them. We are treated like irritants at best and idiots at worst. The ECB appear to regard advocates of the longer game, the primacy of which we can argue non-stop and for hours, as quixotic and eccentrically fuddy-duddy. The ECB also patronises us by trying to pretend that the Championship is sincerely 'very important' and 'significant' to them. Whenever I hear or read that disingenuous claim, it reminds me that the purpose of 'political language' really is to make 'murder sound respectable and to give an appearance of solidity to pure wind'.

I have learned to like Twenty20 – albeit in a far different, far less committed way than I do the Championship. I prefer to view it from the sofa, instead of sitting in a stand, saving me from the sort of spectator who thinks of it as a beer festival with some cricket attached. He will arrive belatedly with a pint in hand and go to and fro from his seat for more of them. George Bernard Shaw once griped about a patron who turned up for an opera at Covent Garden after it had already begun. She sat in his line of sight and exited long before the fat lady sang. 'I do not complain of her coming late and going early,' he said. 'On the contrary. I wish she had come later and left earlier.' I know how Bernard Shaw felt. That is why I would always rather watch a Championship match on a windswept April morning, when almost no one else is around, than go to a Twenty20 slog-fest under lights on a hot August night.

The Hundred, about as appealing to me as a lukewarm bath, is something else entirely. It is so far removed from 'proper cricket' as to be only tangentially connected to the traditions of the game. The future tends to outwit all attempts at accurate prediction; our supposedly intelligent deductions about it are only ever elaborate guesswork. So I don't know whether The Hundred will flop or flourish. I do know that a very old and awfully hoary argument still holds true: no one ever went broke underestimating the taste of the public. The claim is more valid today than when the line originally surfaced and caught on, soon becoming a staple in books of quotations. I see it lit up across social media, a platform where rationality and perspective die voiceless. Also reflecting public taste, like a full-length mirror, is the pap of reality television. Neither it nor Twitter seems to have much in common with The Hundred – until you understand that the ECB is betting the whole house on persuading the same kind of audience to watch a version of the game played nowhere else. The strategy of preaching to the unconverted is high-wire because the ECB

is essentially chasing the youth market, which has been noto-
riously fickle ever since social historians first recognised its
existence. That was in the 1950s. Fads and fashions came and
went then, but the pace of change was glacial compared to
today's, the process now occurring almost hourly. Even if it
catches on, The Hundred will still have to last in a world
constantly being reinvented. If it doesn't, the game faces rid-
icule, which it could survive, and financial calamity, which it
might not.

The ECB will have the BBC as collaborators beside Sky.
The corporation hasn't shown live cricket since 1999, but the
brevity of The Hundred – no match will exceed three hours
in length – is attractive to them. It can be dropped into an
evening schedule without greatly disrupting other programmes
or shoved on to the red button.

Promoting the Championship usually amounts to sticking
up a poster – it looks like a variety bill from the heyday of the
music hall – on the perimeter wall of a ground. Promoting
The Hundred will be a ballyhoo production of colour, hype,
glitter, juggling and raucous fairground barking. We will get
the lot – music, graphics, flashing images – to entice us to roll
up for the circus. The BBC will do it to justify their invest-
ment. Sky will do it because it always does.

I worry, apparently much more than the ECB does, at what
will be lost and soon become irrecoverable as a consequence.

The Championship, already shrunken and diminished, is
the competition always forced to accommodate every other

without complaint. In 1959, everyone played 28 games. In 1969, it was 24. This chipping away went slowly on: 22 by 1989; 17 a decade later; 16 in 2000 after one division was split into two (the equivalent of creating first- and second-class compartments of travel). In 2017, the Championship, pared down to a skinny 14 matches apiece, got shoved further into the background. In 2020, it is intended to be so lopsided – ten teams at the top and eight below them – that some counties in Division One won't even play everyone twice, a throwback to a very different and slightly distant era. Since the Championship starts before all the daffodils have surfaced and ends when the conkers are being collected, we'd better hope the weather is exceptional from far north to deep south and across to the west too. Otherwise the pennant and the Lord's Taverners's Chalice will be determined more than ever by the lottery that Mother Nature draws.

The Hundred is more than just a little reorganisation of the summer's furniture. It is a reinvention of the domestic English game. What lies immediately ahead for the Championship isn't necessarily extinction but is certainly marginalisation, which is the second-worst fate that can befall it. Fading into irrelevance can only be next. And, since uncertainty always follows upheaval, it is neither presumptuous nor scaremongering to fret about what will happen if the novelty of The Hundred quickly wears off or gradually fades.

The ECB reacts with cold dismissiveness and even shock towards anyone lacking rah-rah enthusiasm for the new baby.

In this regard, it behaves rather like the Duke of Wellington, appalled by the effrontery of his cabinet. Swapping the battlefield for Downing Street, Wellington was aghast at what he considered to be rank insubordination at the end of his first meeting with ministers. 'Extraordinary affair,' he wailed. 'I gave them their orders and they wanted to stay and discuss them.' The ECB didn't want to consult where The Hundred was concerned either. We were simply told the game was moving on and we would have to accompany it. Whatever our reservations, and however much we blanched, we were expected to fall in and get behind the ECB for the sake of cricket's future prosperity.

No, thank you.

On that January afternoon, after I'd finished looking wistfully at the Championship fixtures, I thought about the advice John Arlott once gave me about tackling the melancholia of that dead month. He liked to go to his library, pick a title and then turn the pages randomly, finding passages that would carry him into previous summers. I can't tell you how many cricket books I own – thousands upon thousands. Books on shelves of white wood. Books in boxes hidden in deep cupboards. Books, stacked a little unsteadily, that rise and fall like a range of ragged mountains. Books propped against walls. Books sitting beside armchairs or on tables.

Call it serendipity; for the dictionary definition of that word certainly applies. I found a book that, in truth, I had half-forgotten. It was tucked in a corner and dusty along its top edges. I opened it on page 74, which is the start of chapter seven. I read about the pleasure of being at a match well before the first ball is bowled, instantly recognising myself in the following description:

> *You arrive early, even earlier than you meant*
> *. . . and you feel a little guilty at the thought of*
> *the day you propose to deliver up to sheer luxury.*

I began moving indiscriminately backwards and forwards in the text. I checked what the bookselling trade abstractly refers to as the 'front matter'. This revealed it was first published in 1944. The book would 'celebrate' a seventy-fifth anniversary in the year ahead, an occasion I was sure would slip by unheralded. I looked up the author; he had been dead for forty-five years. Irrespective of its age and its relative obscurity, the book spoke especially of things to which the modern reader could relate.

It was Edmund Blunden's *Cricket Country*.

The Second World War had reached into 1942. With the benefit of hindsight, we identify it as the mid-point of the fighting. But the events of that year, which are history for those of us fortunate enough not to have experienced them, counted on the home front as breaking news, delivered daily on the BBC or on the front pages of newspapers mostly comprising only a few sheets of dense type and the odd smudgy photograph. The war was interminable then, the end of it unforeseeable.

That winter, Edmund Blunden settled down to write about his memories of summers past and pastoral. *Cricket Country* became his 224-page prose poem to what he called 'The King of Games'. Blunden had a lover's infatuation with cricket, which, from boyhood, became almost all-consuming for him. His father, capable of producing 'cunning leg breaks' from 'long musician's fingers', had once bowled K. S. Ranjitsinhji in the nets and thought that anyone who made 'a name' for himself in the County Championship had achieved 'human greatness'.

Blunden never hoped to achieve that. He was only 5 foot 4 inches tall and scrawny looking. He was a good-cum-capable cricketer only up to a certain point, never entirely successful and seldom stylish. He nonetheless played with pluck almost every week, primarily as a wicketkeeper-batsman, and acted as though cricket was his true vocation. The rustic abilities Blunden possessed – he often batted without gloves – were liberally spread too, his loyalties shared among an assortment of village teams and club sides, the distinguished and the rag-tag alike. One of them was Heytesbury, under the captaincy of his friend and fellow poet Siegfried Sassoon, who owned the ground on which games were staged because his country house stood on it. Another was The Barnacles, based at Merton College, where Blunden was a Fellow and taught

English literature, the most 'undonnish Oxford don' imaginable.

Blunden begins *Cricket Country* with an explanation of why he is writing it. He says that 'one morning before the world was at war again' he unexpectedly received a poem in the post. The opening lines asked him this question:

> *Have you ever felt the urge to write*
> *Of all the cricket that has blessed your sight?*

Blunden was nudging 43. He was as vulnerable to being wooed as any unhappily married, middle-aged man would be. Of course, he succumbed to the 'gracefully flattering' tone of the poem. And, of course, he was shyly coy with the reader about revealing who wrote it. She was Claire Poynton, the future Mrs Blunden. She was a cricket fan, a member of Lancashire. She was also 22 years younger than him.

Blunden said he could make no 'practical response' to her idea because the war and the 'overwhelming shadows' it cast swallowed everything for him. Not until 'the burden' of them began to lift was Blunden able to consider the proposal.

Even though the war was turning towards the Allies by then, Blunden used *Cricket Country* to shelter from the worst of it. It was a safe haven in which he could lose himself. In letters between him and Sassoon, the two friends mourn the loss of cricket: the players who have gone off to fight – some of them soon to die; the patchwork teams assembled for a scratchy game; a pitch cratered by a stray bomb; air strokes practised with a well-used bat in front of the bedroom mirror; a back issue of *The Cricketer* pulling them into the hot and casually carefree days of the 1930s. Blunden and Sassoon longed only for this: 'To share a comfortable partnership at Heytesbury again . . .' As early as 1941, Blunden says optimistically to Sassoon, 'As in the last war, cricket feels far away but will come again'. I can't read *Cricket Country* without thinking that he didn't quite believe this and would never do so until it actually happened. The significance of the phrase 'as in the last war' also needs no emphasis for anyone who knows the faintest thing about Blunden. Looking very young and very blond, his hair sharply parted, he enlisted at nineteen and fought across all those places on the map that could collectively be renamed Hell: Passchendaele, the Somme, Ypres. Afterwards he wrote *Undertones of War*, a masterpiece of eyewitness reportage. It recorded the horrific sights and the blood stench of the Front, which Blunden could never purge from his thoughts. That book was no catharsis for the author. Ghosts and survivor guilt 'haunted' him until his last breath. When Peter Jackson took the black-and-white newsreels of the war and dipped them in colour, making *They Shall Not Grow Old* to mark the centenary of the Armistice, Blunden's voice – unidentified until the credits appeared – was one of those chosen to accompany images that came at you with such visceral power.

You have to think of *Cricket Country* sitting on the shelf

next to *Undertones of War*, a half-brother of sorts, because Blunden wasn't only thinking about the war that was going on around him as he wrote it. He was also thinking about the previous one. Freshly arrived in France in May 1916, and stuck in a trench there, Blunden tells us in *Cricket Country* how he remembered that the new season ought to have 'just begun'. He then looked at the muddy desolation around him and 'the thought' of cricket 'died in me almost as soon as it was born'. Blunden could not bring himself to read those copies of *Wisden* that were published from 1914 to 1918 until he finally began work on *Cricket Country*. When he did, he said, 'the figures and the narrative mocked me . . . they had a dead look'.

Blunden allowed himself the indulgence of what he called 'a roving commission' on the book's behalf. He defined it as 'a winding and sometimes tangled path'. *Cricket Country* is consequently profoundly discursive as well as tenderly elegiac. Blunden purposefully switched the narrative into reflections about poetry and art. He did so because he regarded cricket as inseparable from his other aesthetic pursuits. He also wanted to relate the game to the context of life and plant it in the English landscape. When Blunden talks about 'a lost sunburnt pasture', he isn't only thinking about the village oval, where oaks and elms mark the boundary and the pavilion is a rickety shed. He is evoking rural life around it: farm carts and horse-drawn carriages; thatched cottages and pubs with black beams and brass; hedgerows and wheat fields and dusty pathways; the roll of grassy hills and wild flowers and thick woodland.

Though born in London, on Tottenham Court Road, Blunden's cricketing heart was split between the competing counties of the South-east. 'In our village and our county, the game was so native, so constant, so beloved without fuss that it came to me as the air I breathed,' he said. 'Our village' was Yalding in Kent. Blunden grew up among its abundant hop-fields and orchards and beside three rivers, the Teise and the Beult slipping into the fat Medway. At the weekend, the fellows who cut the hay would swap their agricultural labourers' clothes for cricket whites.

For Blunden, cricket's 'unique magnetism' stemmed from the fact it was a 'contest of a number of abilities and possibilities'. The game was 'a science' and also 'a wheel of fortune and a drama of personalities and intentions'. He maintained the tactics and intricate technical nuances, making a match like multi-dimensional chess, turned watching into an 'intellectual exercise'. It brought 'mental fascination' that could 'exhaust' you, he added.

Cricket, he explained, was his 'earthly paradise', and his book respectfully bows in front of players he considers worthy, such as W. G. Grace and C. B. Fry, Colin Blythe and The Big Ship, Warwick Armstrong. Blunden memorably sketches Armstrong's well-upholstered bulk in the manner of Swift depicting Gulliver in Lilliput; he made 'a bat look like a tea spoon and the bowling weak tea'. Blunden was besotted with

Len Hutton, so cherishing a photograph of 'the marvellous boy' that he framed and hung it over his mantelpiece. He is shaking hands with Donald Bradman at The Oval in 1938. Blunden had been there to follow, run-by-run, Hutton's world-record score of 364, an achievement of sweat, superhuman stamina and splendid shot-making.

His worship of Walter Hammond was conveyed in poetry:

> *Not to have seen him leaves us unaware*
> *What cricket swiftness, judgment, foresight, truly are.*

And *Cricket Country* has barely got off the mark when he devotes a long paragraph in memoriam to 'the genius and character' of Hedley Verity, who died in Sicily after a blast of shrapnel buried itself in his chest. He was 'tall and well-poised', unforgettable to whoever saw him 'trust in the fine art of his cricket'.

However much the professionals and gentlemen amateurs of the Championship drew him through the gates at Lord's and The Oval or at Hove and Canterbury, Blunden's beautiful eye for the game always turned homeward, alighting on the places where his infatuation had first begun.

It seems unlikely to us today – since you assume other offers would have carried more lustre and been more lucrative for him – but George Orwell wrote a weekly column about books in the *Manchester Evening News*. It was Blunden's immense good fortune that Orwell took on that assignment only four months before *Cricket Country* arrived in the shops. Some big hitters queued up to review it. Notable among them were R. C. Robertson-Glasgow, almost rivalling Neville Cardus in popularity and respect, and L. P. Hartley, who would go on to write *The Go-Between*. Orwell's is still the most significant critique. He maintained that cricket was a peculiar beast. 'Either you like it or you don't,' he said. He hovered somewhere between those polar opposites; while not wholly antagonistic, he wasn't entirely warm towards it either. His astute angle of approach burrowed to the core of the book and also to Blunden himself. 'Mr Blunden is a true cricketer,' declared Orwell. 'The test of a true cricketer is that he shall prefer village cricket to "good cricket".' He noted his 'due reverence for the famous figures', but then looked beyond that. It was 'obvious', said Orwell, that Blunden's 'friendliest memories are of village cricket . . . where everyone plays in braces, where the blacksmith is liable to be called away mid-innings on an urgent job, and sometimes, about the time the light begins to fail, a ball driven for four kills a rabbit on the boundary'.

As far as Blunden was concerned, the village provided the foundation on which the rest of English cricket was constructed. He most preferred those games with 'lots of beer and cheerfulness in a field opposite the village church'. What awakened his empathy was always the underdog and the conscientious but untalented enthusiast. He eulogised 'the ever unsuccessful player' who 'comes up afresh for execution' before every match, the sort who 'came to the crease in faultless flannels but without any hope'. He went on: 'I have known cricketers who, as far as my observation went, practically never scored a run, nor were called on to bowl, nor took much part in the rest of the proceedings, and yet they were always present, always eager.' Nothing, added Blunden, was 'relished more' than the sight of someone forced to wield the bat inadequately at number eleven with only 'the help of Heaven' to get him a run. Sassoon seized on those descriptions too. After getting hold of the book, he reported back to Blunden: 'I felt it all . . . the wet ball retrieved from the long grass beyond the wood.'

I was affected most by the passages that were ostensibly only about cricket, but in reality were also about the character of the game and the very Englishness of it. I began to imagine Blunden writing the book with the steel-tipped dip pen that he always used and a pot of black ink, the pages accumulating gradually in his rooms at Merton. Nowadays, most of us can scarcely put down half a dozen decently neat lines before our hand begins to ache and sentences spread into a spidery tangle, hopelessly uneven and soon illegible. Schooled in a far different era, the best of Blunden's handwriting counts almost as calligraphy. Once seen, it is not forgotten. The generous downward loop of his *g*s and *y*s. The way the cross of his *t*, whenever he writes *at*, slopes into a steep bridge that connects to the first letter of the next word. The elaborate architecture of an *h* and the upward curve of an *f*. He wrote the way he wanted to bat, which was with a flourish.

When I read *Cricket Country* for the first time, which was three decades or so ago, it struck me as being about the comfort of memory. That was a naïve conclusion to make. Reading the book again, which I did with a deliberate slowness, I realised something else about it. Blunden is not only stressing what cricket has meant to him; he is expressing what it ought to mean to us too. His affinity with the game is demonstrated in the love and the nostalgia he feels for it. Blunden frankly concedes that cricket is 'ever-changeful'. He also admits that 'even among the English' it is seen as 'the prime English eccentricity'. But he thinks it is worth preserving. And, more significantly, he is letting us know what should last of it in case war means nothing much does. You could dismiss him as daftly romantic, but – just as the rest of us do from time to time – he is only wishing to have again something that had once seemed his for ever. Blunden has a wider purpose still for dwelling on this. He is showing us how bereft we will be if, one summer morning, we find that the game as we know it has gone.

I can relate to that now.

Surprisingly, Blunden never gave us a sequel to *Cricket Country*. He did, however, write a piece for the *Strand*. It appeared a year after the book's publication. He detected a 'sense' that cricket was 'losing its supremacy as the national game' to football and regretted the attitude of those who found it 'too slow'. He thought 'a shade of grief' was 'falling over this old country game'. With more trepidation still,

Blunden forecast that 'proposals for a Cricket Cup and a knock out competition' could be introduced as a solution. His prediction was not fulfilled for another eighteen years, but the warning tacked on to it is relevant and evergreen. 'Cricket', he said, 'does not depend upon expedients, nor can it live by attempts to imitate the rhythm, the dash and the shock of football.' Were he living now, aware of The Hundred, he would be writing a letter to the ECB to remind them of that, his handwriting as gorgeous as ever. If it bothered to reply at all, the ECB would fob him off with some standard, contemptuous flannel about a five-year plan and the growth spurt the game could undergo. It seems to make up these responses as it goes along, never satisfactorily explaining how the Championship will successfully coexist, let alone remain roughly intact, with the white-ball competitions around it.

I felt a special companionship with Blunden, a connection between us made because of the way he looked at cricket then and the way I look at cricket now. It may seem trite and somewhat out of proportion to invoke *Cricket Country* and then draw parallels from it. Blunden was acting in response to human catastrophe. I act only at a point of radical change in the game. It is, nonetheless, profoundly unsettling to those of us who believe it could be irreversible. Blunden once thought that cricket was 'immortal and inevitable' because there was 'plenty' around of the sort he wanted to watch. I wish I could say the same now. The

Championship is being reduced to a scale model of the thing it used to be. At the present rate of erosion, the only place it will exist, twenty or thirty years from now, is in the record books.

I know those of a conservative disposition are never sanguine about innovation and will always rage against it. Opposition to the Gillette Cup, as well as the John Player League, produced strident wailing that was soon muted.

The Hundred feels different from either of those competitions. Neither forced the whole summer to be overhauled. Neither was prioritised above the Championship. The Gillette Cup found a midweek slot between three-day matches. The John Player League filled previously unoccupied Sundays – a Sabbath when shops were shut, pubs opened only for a few hours and afternoons were somnolently spent with the day's newspapers or the black-and-white movie matinee on BBC1.

The Hundred will land on top of the game like a grand piano falling from space.

Jeetan Patel, back in the ground where his career
in England improbably began.

CHAPTER TWO

Superior Mortals and Superheroes

The ghosts of Peel and Hawke. A player called Kitcat.
The peripatetic cricketer. Tendulkar in the nets. The secret
Brian Close shared. The Man Who Made the Catch.

The tourists, predominantly Japanese, are milling about the Minster as early as 9.15 a.m. and admiring its formidable beauty. With time to spare and no promises to keep, I am milling about with them. I watch a family of four stop a passer-by who is carrying a mustard-coloured rucksack. They hand him a Nikon camera and gesture politely towards the top step of the Great West Door, the arch so gorgeous that it could be the grand entrance to Heaven itself. The family gathers tightly together beneath the ornate tracery and the numerous niche figures carved into the magnesian limestone, the soft rich colour of which always lightens, as if diluted, when splashed by the sun. The souvenir photograph is smartly taken and then smiles and bows and a thumbs-up are traded in gratitude. The spoken 'Thank you' accompanying them, which comes from the father, is guttural and slightly mispronounced. He takes back the Nikon and starts clicking madly away at the façade of the Minster, as though afraid of missing a square centimetre of detail. He leans extravagantly backwards, capturing the towers and their fine high finials against the hard blue of the morning sky, and is soon wandering about to capture the buttresses, the gargoyles and the splendour of the stained glass too.

I am tempted to tell him that something else, also worthy of being photographed, is happening in York today. He won't have to travel far to get to it either. To reach Clifton Park, he'd need only to turn around and walk a little over a mile in a fairly straightish line. True, the pavilion is not a splendid architectural amalgam of the Gothic and the Perpendicular. It is less than a decade old, minimal and boxy. You could draw the whole thing with so few strokes that the point of a freshly sharpened pencil would scarcely be blunted. True, also, is the fact that you have to use the raw materials of your imagination to make the landscape around it especially appealing. There are pleasant trees and some low shrubbery; particularly fine are a big oak and two tall, flourishing white poplars, their splayed branches heavy with leaf. There is a handsomely weathered brick wall that ought to border an Edwardian Arts and Crafts garden, choked with roses and foxgloves, delphiniums and herbaceous borders. All of us should have bought shares in the marquee business this summer, so ubiquitous has the appearance of a tent or two on a first-class cricket field become. There is enough white canvas on display at Clifton Park to have sailed Nelson's fleet at Trafalgar. But no one would come to this modern corner of medieval York to swoon over the way it looks. What has drawn the crowds this week is the rarity of the event being staged here. Yorkshire, third in the table, are facing Warwickshire, second from bottom, in the County Championship.

I think about selling the match as a curiosity to the Japanese family; something idiosyncratic and historic in a small-world way. Not to be missed because you can't be certain when – or if – the like of it will ever be seen again. I could explain that in 1890, at Wigginton Road, posters were advertising 'A Grand Match' between Yorkshire and Kent. I could add that the *Yorkshire Post* and *Leeds Intelligencer* tactfully reported the farce that occurred before it even began. Kent, it said, found themselves in a 'very awkward predicament'. Their team arrived with only eight players. No doubt the absentees caught the nineteenth-century equivalent of Virgin's Super Voyager train and came to a shrieking halt somewhere outside Doncaster. Whatever the reason, which was never adequately explained, the scorecard recorded the missing as being 'absent hurt'. Kent won the toss and had no option but to bat first in 'terribly dark weather'. Yorkshire bowled them out for 46; ten of those runs were extras. The Kent side included the estimable Lord

Harris, President of the MCC only five years later, and the Hearne brothers, George and Alec. Yorkshire were led by their patriarch-cum-cricketing impresario Lord Hawke, who mobilised a very unruly bunch and sent them into war. Much later and elsewhere, Hawke would fall out spectacularly with his chief strike bowler Bobby Peel over the question of whether Peel, rotted by drink, had or had not used a sight screen the way a dog uses a lamppost. Against Kent, however, Peel was perfectly sober and sublimely unplayable. He took four wickets in the first innings and five in the second, giving him match figures of nine for 48; Kent got a walloping.

The county never used Wigginton Road for a Championship fixture again. It had a valid excuse for not doing so only from the end of the 1960s. The ground was dug up so a hospital could be built on the site. Yorkshire's return to York took 129 years and seven days. Just like Sookholme, Clifton Park has a gig at last because of the World Cup. England face Sri Lanka at Headingley at the end of the week.

Of course, I say none of this to the father and his family. At his urgent beckoning – it's as if he is worried the city walls will collapse before he sees them – he marches his wife and children away, turns a corner and disappears down a cobbled street.

It is the game's last day. Yorkshire begin their second innings 178 for seven, only 183 in front and desperate for the tail to wag rather than sag.

I settle down on the grey wooden bench that is fixed to the brick wall at the base of the scoreboard. I have a view over the shoulder of long on. Yorkshire are tentative and a little terrified at first, the task of building a decent lead and getting the bowlers to defend it already daunting for them. Sorely in need of another hundred runs at least, Yorkshire make just 33 from 18 overs, each of which is all about holding their ground rather than advancing their position. Only Jack Leaning, who makes a doughty 62, has much fight in him.

The opening hour is so dour and insipid that I begin to flick through the slick, 28-page commemorative brochure, which York Cricket Club are selling around the boundary for £5. I am fond of photographs of Victorian cricketers, flesh-and-blood men who seem so different from us but are actually so alike. The run-makers among them use plain bats that are no more than shavings of wood. The bowlers stand in bulky boots, like a coalminer's. The wicketkeepers wear gloves that resemble factory gauntlets, fit for dragging steel out of a furnace. I am especially smitten with one figure – Sidney Kitcat, who played for Gloucestershire between the end of the nineteenth century and the beginning of the twentieth. It isn't only that his name tickles me. In a posed photograph, which I own, Kitcat crouches at the crease like a contortionist trying to fold himself perfectly in half. His grip on the bat's long handle suggests his 1,800-odd runs predominantly came through mid-wicket. His unorthodoxy makes him seem faintly preposterous. His gimlet gaze and his expression of utter seriousness give Kitcat the look of an explorer too, the kind of fellow who would intrepidly go forth to some unknown outpost off the map at the drop of a pit helmet.

In York CC's glossy brochure, I come across black-and-white postcard-sized portraits of Bobby Peel and Lord Hawke, and also the wan faces of Yorkshire's team from 1893. All of them wore caps adorned with the white rose. All, it seems, used black belts to hold up their cream flannels. Anyone without a moustache, sprouting like an unruly privet hedge, counted as being improperly dressed. You can nowadays download a free online tool to transform monochrome photographs into colour, bringing out the definition in them in the same way that polish brings out the grain in wood. These shots are better left untouched. You realise, staring into Peel's eyes, each of which is like the black dot at the heart of a Flanders poppy, how short was cricket's Arcadian Golden Age and also how long ago it ended.

As the ground fills around me, I start to think not about Peel and the past, but the future instead. If the County Championship seriously has one, it is in places such as Clifton Park. My neighbour believes so too. He is wrapped in a red scarf and a fawn cardigan with a shawl collar. His thin silvery hair is swept back. He has been watching the Championship for 'almost 60 years', he explains. He'd once gone wherever Yorkshire travelled in the county. He'd seen them play in the West, the East and the South Ridings. Coming to York was like getting, at last, the one sticker he needed to complete a collector's album. We agree that Clifton Park has a pleasant, festival-like air about it. We agree that it has a rich soil on which a Championship game ought to be played regularly, leaving Headingley to stage Test matches and the white-ball malarkey under floodlights. We also agree – after our conversation unexpectedly meanders in an entirely different direction – that one reason we cherish cricket is its ethnic diversity.

We are watching Jeetan Patel bowl wilily to James Logan, finally getting rid of him. Logan went to cut and found Patel had disguised some extra pace in his delivery, which brought him some extra lift too; Logan lost his off bail. The 39-year-old off-spinner from Wellington had instructed the 21-year-old slow-armer from Wakefield in the basics of his craft. The game marks a homecoming for Patel. He spent his debut summer in England at York in 2003. The club benefited from it almost as much as he did. Patel picked up 40 wickets at a little over 21 apiece, maturing over those months as a character as well as a cricketer. 'Great life experience' is how he describes it now. My new friend and I discuss how Patel, the son of Indian parents but born in New Zealand, has enriched the Championship like so many overseas players before him.

I was lucky. I discovered the game just as the Championship began importing talent, principally from the West Indies. The importance of this only became apparent to me retrospectively; I was too young to be aware of it while the thing was happening. Early on, I took for granted the fact that my pocket money, which was only a few shillings, enabled me to watch Clive Lloyd or Majid Khan, Farokh Engineer or Rohan Kanhai, who would sometimes bat in a white neckerchief and with his shirt cuffs casually unbuttoned. I took for granted, too, the way in which I could make easy conversation with smart-suited gents who had sailed here on the *Windrush*, the ship's funnels like stubby factory chimneys coughing smoke. Or that whole families, their postal addresses formerly in cities such as Bombay or Karachi, would politely offer to share their lunch with a waif without food who was sitting alone. With no sense of history, I thought nothing of that gesture. Colour was irrelevant. Creed was irrelevant also. We were all warming our hands over the same fire, which cricket had lit. I naïvely assumed cricket-watching had always been like this – and so had England.

I was twelve years old when a teacher read E. R. Braithwaite's *To Sir With Love* to the class. I can quote the opening line still: 'The crowded red double-decker bus inches its way through the snarl of traffic in Aldgate.' The book is about Braithwaite, a West Indian, teaching in an east London school. He'd been a Royal Air Force pilot during the Second World War. He'd earned a master's degree at Cambridge. After being demobbed, he got stuck in numerous dead ends nonetheless. Braithwaite wrote: 'I had just been brought face to face with something I had either forgotten or completely ignored for more than six exciting years – my black face.' I realised properly only then that everyone who had briefly befriended me at cricket matches surely suffered racial abuse too and did so without being able to complain about it.

I announce all this to my neighbour on the bench. Another spectator, silent until then, chips in with his own three-penn'orth. He still possessed his whites and his boots, he said. He still owned a bat too. He liked to play peripatetically, content to be a guest at the eleventh hour for teams who suddenly found themselves a man down (Lord Harris would have found him useful in 1890). He didn't necessarily care whether he batted or bowled or was sent to graze at long leg during one over and waved towards the cover boundary for the next. He revelled in the friendships he made, the camaraderie of the dressing room. 'I go to enjoy myself,' he added. His body was trim but hardly athletic. His face was creased in all the predictable places. I spontaneously asked him his age. 'I'm 70,' he said. His interruption sounded oddly ungermane. It was as though he'd misheard what we'd been talking about and, as a consequence, had completely misunderstood the line of our debate. That judgment turned out to be presumptuous and very stupid. One of the teams for which he played had the suffix 'Methodists', he told us. His story, built slowly, had reached its point. 'The thing is, there are hardly any Methodists in it. Most of the lads are Muslim. No one cares a bit and never has.' On he went, anxious to add a further piece of evidence. 'When I watched Sachin Tendulkar for the first time – and that was *nearly* 30 years ago – I saw a young lad who looked an authentic *player*. I wanted to go back and watch him again as soon as I could. We all thought that way, didn't we? That's the sort of game cricket is, isn't it? We're never bothered where anyone comes from, are we? It just isn't important.'

He turns to follow the next ball; Patel has started a new over. Except to express my jealousy that he still goes into the field every weekend, while I'd long since become a sedentary non-combatant, I have nothing substantial to add. But a butterfly thought floats past me; it is about Tendulkar.

It was an impulsive journey, the decision taken rashly last-minute, and in a panic, as though I was afraid of changing my mind even at the planning stage.

I nearly did.

At the station, watching the train pull in, I hesitated before meeting it, questioning all the time whether this was a fool's errand, the daftest of mistakes. I totted up the cost of the ticket and the bed and breakfast, both booked randomly and cheaply, and almost wrote them off, like a bad debt. There were few seats. There was also an ungainly jostle among passengers frantic to claim them. There was the slam of heavy carriage doors. There was a guard with a whistle, glancing along the platform. There was the tannoy announcement, urging the stragglers to hurry. And so, in the end, I climbed aboard, somewhat reluctantly. As the train jolted forward, I looked at the spot where I'd just been standing, half-expecting to find myself still there.

July was about to fall into August, but the weather had been lousy for a couple of days. So had I. That is why, a long weekend stretching ahead, I had decided to make the trip without telling anyone. The whim on which it was made disguised a little desperation. Every turning I made in life seemed to be the wrong one then. Often, the old Black Dog meant there was no recognisable shape to my life; everything was warped somehow, like your reflection in a fairground mirror. Heading to Worcester to watch Sachin Tendulkar was my search for a cure. Having successfully used cricket as a pharmacy before, I was doing so again.

India were a week away from the second Test, which would be Tendulkar's 98th. He was 29, routinely scoring colossal hundreds. But his form in England that midsummer had been wretched. His previous three scores were 3, 16 and 12, the sort of miserable totals a novice darts player would chalk up on the pub board. I'd even read a few peculiar mutterings about whether the burden of being the breadwinner had become too much for Tendulkar, the responsibility buckling him.

Rain had soaked New Road for the previous 48 hours. Not a ball had been bowled in the game. There was a photograph of Tendulkar staring forlornly at the covers and the sodden outfield from behind pavilion glass. His expression was pensive but slightly beseeching, as though silently asking for a break. He sorely needed a minimum of three sessions in the middle; his strokes had rusted and Time was the only oil that would unstick them. The weather forecast for day three, a Friday, was encouraging. I was also convinced that Tendulkar would come out of his rut to greet the sun. Donald Bradman once declared: 'I don't believe in the Law of Averages'. I do. I *knew* Tendulkar would claim a big score.

The following morning, I walked to the ground. The route took me past the cathedral, past the bronze statue of Elgar, hands clasped behind his back and past the swans paddling against the flow of the dirty-brown Severn, its banks swollen by the week's rain. Tendulkar was walking into the nets, generously timing his arrival almost exactly with mine. It was as if he'd been expecting me and had decided to wait.

Cricket always offers the chance to get so close to a player you admire; it can feel as though you are both occupying the same space. As a boy, I once stood so dangerously near to a net that I had to take evasive action when John Edrich pugnaciously clipped a ball my way. I saw it late and had to dodge it abruptly. If I hadn't, I would still have the imprint of the maker's name embossed on my forehead. Edrich courteously came over to ask about my wellbeing. I had learned my lesson. From a safer distance, where a tin hat wasn't required, I saw Michael Holding in the nets at Derbyshire. That gorgeously smooth action reminded me of someone uncurling a long bolt of silk with no more than a swish of their arm and a slinky

flick of their wrist. Speed made something that was so beautiful also so devastating. For the unfortunates padded up to
face him, it must have been like a training exercise with live
ammunition. One ball, a blur to the eye, bulged against the
back of the saggy net with such a whoosh that you expected
the pegs holding it to be wrenched loose. This was Holding
merely off a casual trot, carefully restraining himself. I thought
of Brian Close and the livid bruising he got after Holding
thumped short deliveries into him at Old Trafford. I admired
Close's bravery all over again.

My compulsion to watch players practise began when I saw
a rare roll of film of W. G. Grace. The film is brief, jerky, silent
and scratched. Grace is on the outfield, lustily punching back
deliveries from an unseen bowler. He is bulky but not corpulent. His beard needs a barber's scissors to groom it. His
flannels look a bit scruffy. His sun hat, the brim narrow, seems
glued to his head. In the beginning, Grace fascinated me, the
rat-a-tat of his shot-making accentuated by the hand-cranked
camera. Gradually, however, I took more notice of his audience,
a poignant gathering. Behind him sat a couple of boys, one yet
to reach his teens, dressed in Harrow's distinctive school uniform: straw boater, dark suit and waistcoat, with a huge false
collar attached to a white shirt. The film was taken some time
in the 1890s. That is why I can't help but see those boys as
men in far different uniform: two officers marching into the
Great War in 1914. Who were they, and what happened to
them? Did they live to walk upon 'England's pastures green'

again? Did that sunlit afternoon with Grace – the sight of the big man's broad back – return to them on some rainy, muddy day in the trenches? Since 2,917 Harrovians went to that war and 2,335 of them returned, I prefer to think of the boys as survivors, telling the tale of Grace over brandy and Cuban cigars in some swanky London club. I hope that is the truth of it.

I also like to think that somewhere, glimpsed at the edges of a photograph or a clip of film, is the sight of a younger me beside Brian Lara or Ricky Ponting, Shane Warne or Brett Lee, Kumar Sangakkara or Muttiah Muralitharan. Only a year or two ago, watching Lancashire at Southport, those of us who went out to inspect the wicket at tea were treated to the sight of Jimmy Anderson on a nearby strip. He was testing his fitness, bowling against a single stump. Even if that stump could have fought back, it wouldn't have lasted long. Anderson was only 90 per cent himself and, like Holding, he came in off a shortened run. He still made the ball tear up the air, the seam making a ripping sound through it. I was standing where forward short leg would have been, waiting for the inside edge. Someone, at mid-off or thereabouts, was snapping away with a pocket camera. Perhaps I am in a corner of one of those photographs, a studious expression on my face.

There was no film crew to witness Tendulkar in the nets at Worcester. There was no amateur photographer either. I wish there had been. To watch him was like observing a concert pianist tackling his scales before letting go and rattling out a jazz number. The Tendulkar you saw in the middle was replicated there. The perfect V of his grip. The right foot behind the front line of the crease. His head still. His body side-on. The constant readjustment of his box, which seemed to irritate him. He played a lot of forward defensive shots at first, as though wanting to feel the solid slap of the ball against the bat. Then he played a lot of backward defensive shots too, up on his tippy toes. The right hand, slackening at the bottom of the handle, meant the ball landed with a soft plop at his feet. You'd think some obedient dog had presented it to him.

More than a decade later, at a hotel function, I briefly stood back-to-back with Tendulkar and discovered we are almost identical in height and shape. In that net, though, I appreciated how that small bundle – Tendulkar is 5 foot 5 inches tall – understood the physiology of batting as much as the psychology. A low centre of gravity is only an advantage if you know how to use and maximise it. The balance he demonstrated in that neatly compact frame begat the poise in his repertoire of shots.

Tendulkar tackled the net, which lasted half an hour, with absolute concentration until the final ten minutes. He began to drive. He began to cut. He began to demonstrate one of his signature shots – the whip off his pads. He even paddle-swept the odd ball. The innings which followed was a mirror image of all this on a pitch surprisingly firm. Tendulkar didn't get in until noon had come and gone and lunch was approaching. The crowd were impatient for him. He barely survived a hat-trick ball from Gareth Batty, groping for it outside off stump. He fought, not so much against the bowlers but himself, until reaching 50, which was a taut affair. It took him 118 balls. Temperament got him there when his classic technique could not because it was still awry. As it returned, gradually, his century (the 53rd of his first-class career) came up in only another 76 deliveries. The 50 or so runs that followed – he made 169 in total – came from a varied parade of stroke-making. It seemed as though – through telepathy, no doubt –Tendulkar knew where the ball would pitch as soon as the bowler turned on his mark and began running in. The scorebook tells me that he hit 30 fours. I know one of them, an uppish square cut, nearly put a hole in the pavilion fence. Another was off-driven slightly on the up; I am sure anyone else would have prodded at it. A third, executed most suavely, was a wristy leg-side clip that went to the rope before you'd even registered it had actually left the bat.

New Road, sparsely populated in the morning, began to fill, the weekend starting prematurely for workers who had bunked off early because Tendulkar was batting.

As the afternoon wore on, the sun making an appearance, you realised again that, quite simply, there was no one else like him. That Indian team included Sehwag, never a slouch, and also Ganguly and Dravid. But you always wanted Tendulkar on strike and, after he was finally out, you knew home was calling. The game shrank in size when he departed from it.

His innings was a jewel, but I cherish more the preparation for it in that net. I saw there how something was actually made; how, in fact, within a few hours, Tendulkar had gone from being out of form to being in form. I had the satisfaction of knowing that the tough work for it was done while I'd been staring over his shoulder, admiring the panache in his 3lb 2oz bat.

The sky at Clifton Park, which became a washed-out grey shortly before lunch, brightens appreciably again when Warwickshire get stuck into a chase for 217. Their pursuit of it begins cautiously, as if wary that a camouflaged trap has been laid for them somewhere.

If batsmen on opposite sides can ever really be pitched against one another, like boxers in a ring, then this match does it. Gary Ballance already has four hundreds – a 149 and a 159 among them – and two half-centuries. Ballance's last Test appearance for England was in 2017, ending a two-year period in which he was dropped, recalled and dropped again. His approach was poked at, picked over and scrutinised in super-slow motion. His trigger movement of going deep into his crease and across his stumps, successful in the beginning, was deemed unsatisfactory for the top level as soon as bowlers (especially left-armers) began spearing the ball at his pads. There have been whispers about a possible England recall. These seem unlikely to lead to a formal invitation just yet. While Ballance has done repair work on his technique, you nevertheless get the impression that the selectors, tepid towards him, will always have their eyes on where the cracks used to be. The more likely candidate for their blessing is Warwickshire's opener, Dom Sibley, who has two centuries and fell only 13 short of a third. He has written his signature across several matches so far this summer. Clifton Park's is another of them.

Yorkshire know all about Sibley. Aged only 18 years and 21 days, excused from his A-level studies at Whitgift School, he made 242 against them for Surrey and became the County Championship's youngest ever double centurion. Four years later, he swapped The Oval for Edgbaston.

Sibley made 67 in the first innings here, nudging ahead of Ballance's 64. As the afternoon progresses, he leaps ahead of him more commandingly still. Sibley is a beefy lad, six-foot tall, who wears a sleeveless sweater and a short-sleeved shirt, as if to show off his muscles. He biffs the ball hard, particularly to leg. His stance is unconventionally open, giving the bowlers more than a glimpse of the stumps. The toe of his right boot rests between middle and leg. The heel of his left boot is where a fifth or sixth stump would be planted. So when Ben Coad quickly appeals for lbw against Sibley, you know – even if you are sitting at square leg – that all he will hear back is a slightly mocking 'No'.

Warwickshire only reach double figures in the sixth over. It takes a further 14 overs for them to go past 50. The pace begins to accelerate when Will Rhodes, Sibley's opening partner, takes 4, 4, 6, 6 and then another 6 off a Jack Leaning over. When, on 83, he jabs a ball from David Willey on to his stumps – the first Willey has delivered at him from around wicket – Warwickshire are 132 for one. It ought to be a soft-shoe shuffle from here.

Sibley is almost never still. He is either readjusting his pads or pulling at the peak of his blue helmet or wandering in half-circles towards square leg and back again. Even when the ball is about to be bowled, Sibley will sometimes abruptly dip at the knee. It's as though he is ducking out of the way of a bird flying low towards him. He begins to take charge, reaching his half-century. He soon clicks past the 60s and the 70s too, another ton outlined for him on a horizon now very near. But Sibley has made 81 – and Warwickshire are strolling it on 181 for two – when a startling catch uproots him and upsets them. Sibley's lofted drive off James Logan is certain to bring him another boundary; I wait to hear the thud the ball will make when it lands. At mid-off, Steve Patterson, who can look a little stiff and creaky sometimes, soars to his right, intercepts it one-handed and grasps the shot as tightly as a winning lottery ticket.

When, just a couple of hours earlier, that discussion on the wooden bench had ranged so broadly around the question of starry overseas talent and how much the Championship had got out of it, we were thinking primarily of West Indians, Indians, Pakistanis and a smattering of Australians. In today's competition, the dominance of one county over another all too frequently depends on whether your South African Kolpak player is stronger than theirs. The Kolpak ruling, strung together like a spider's web of regulation, allows EU citizens and also citizens of countries that are part of EU Association Agreements to perform in England without the irksome bother of being classified as 'overseas'. As well as Hampshire's Kyle Abbott, destroyer of Nottinghamshire, among the most prominent of them this season are Morne Morkel at Surrey, Colin Ackermann at Leicestershire, David Wiese at Sussex and the all-rounder Simon Harmer at Essex. The migrants get accused of being motivated solely by mercenary intent – the rand is puny against the pound – but the English stage is also much more inviting because it is bigger and the light it casts is brighter. Yorkshire's Kolpak recruit is the quick bowler Duanne Olivier, the 43rd such player to hitch himself to an English county. He signed his contract, aged 26, after taking 48 wickets in ten Tests for South Africa; he wants to qualify for England in 2023. Olivier, capable of reaching speeds in the mid-80s, has a hip injury and is side-lined, *hors du combat*.

Had he been here, the day could have been very different. The next 45 minutes prove that.

We are never so impressionable as when we are young. Early devotions stay with us like first love, never forgotten. But I can't imagine today's generation of cricket fanatics, about to have The Hundred unleashed on them, will follow a Kolpak signing with the fervour and devotion that my generation followed the pioneer overseas players of the late 1960s and throughout the 1970s.

Because Trent Bridge was only a 15-minute bus ride away from where I lived, and because Nottinghamshire had signed the best cricketer of the lot, my hero – then and still – was Garry Sobers.

I worked with Jonny Bairstow on the book that became his autobiography, *A Clear Blue Sky*. We differed on nothing but this: he thought the game's greatest all-rounder was Jacques Kallis; I was Sobers's passionate advocate, implacably sure that I possessed the stronger argument. For me, Kallis qualifies as a superior mortal. Sobers was other-worldly. We very amicably agreed to disagree with one another, which confirmed something for me: how difficult it is to convince one generation, which was inconveniently born too late to witness it, about the merits of another.

Sobers only had to walk out of the pavilion gate for the spotlight to settle on him. He did so with both a loose-limbed insouciance and a kind of upper-class hauteur. When he was batting, no one moved from their seat. When he was out, you'd look around and see heads droop in genuine sadness or mortification; the day had got a little dimmer. There was a great calm about him, but his innings were pyrotechnical, fizz and colour in nearly every stroke. Sobers might only be at the crease for an hour or less, but he got into the 50s and even the 70s at a rate that suggested he had a sly eye on the clock because of a rendezvous for which he daren't be late. Genius doesn't abide by everyday rules and practices. Eventually I learnt that Sobers's preparation for his cavalier innings usually involved watching a nag on TV, perhaps racing at Haydock or Kempton Park, before he picked up – casually and at random – one of the half dozen or so Slazenger bats that were propped beside the rest of his kit. If only it was that simple for everyone . . .

He could play the most remarkable shot, but still have the look of someone only vaguely satisfied with his work. It was good, he thought, but could be better.

We always think first about the runs Sobers scored so explosively without paying as much attention to his bowling. He took 235 wickets in Tests alone. The wicketkeeper Deryck Murray, who saw most of them from the sharp end, told me that Sobers was 'faster than most people gave him credit for'. Coming from someone whose hands were raw from taking what Michael Holding sent his way, this was worthy of being written down like court evidence. Murray knew the difference between someone authentically quick and someone who just had a bit of nip about them.

Sobers's stellar statistics – there were 1,043 first-class wickets – ought to come with an asterisk pointing you towards a lengthy footnote. For he was not just one type of bowler. I saw him bowl fast. I saw him cut down his pace to generate profound swing in overcast and muggy conditions. I saw him spin the ball both ways. In the latter years of his career, as his knees became fragile, his gait rolled and rocked, but still didn't prevent him from spearheading an attack. Whatever his team needed, he could provide it. Murray said something else to me too. Sobers was good enough as a wicketkeeper to have stood in a Test.

He would regularly appear near the top of the county averages when Notts were near the bottom of the Championship table. Even the man who could do anything, and often did it so extraordinarily, couldn't entirely bear the lead weight of the team around him. Notts made the mistake of thinking he alone would be sufficient to transform them. Sobers had a face full of feeling and, occasionally, it would betray a smidgen of disillusionment when others couldn't match the standard of his performance.

If I trace my interest in cricket back to its source, as if tracking the flow of a river, I am certain my love for it began with my love of Sobers. But we all think of the 'What ifs' that litter our lives, the roads not taken. What if Sobers had gone to Surrey? Or Warwickshire? Or Lancashire? Without Sobers at Notts, would cricket have cradled me as it did? More than 40 years after watching him for the first time, I learned something revelatory.

Not long before his death, I spent a treasured six hours talking to Brian Close about his career. I asked him about Sobers, knowing he respected and admired him as a person as well as a player. Unlikely as this sounds, Sobers had guested for Yorkshire during a tour of Bermuda during the mid-1960s. Such a bond was formed between them – over the odd tot of alcohol and a mutal fondness for horse racing – that Close wanted to bring his friend to Headingley. He went as far as to clandestinely sound out a few members of the committee, hoping to garner support and then momentum for the proposition. But being born in Barbados, rather than Batley, was a handicap Sobers couldn't overcome. The county, a closed shop, wouldn't countenance breaking the hidebound tradition that only a Yorkshireman could play for Yorkshire. There'd be no exceptions – not even for the world's greatest performer.

The failed coup still rankled with Close decades later because he knew how differently his own future, as well as Yorkshire's, would have turned out. The feast that was theirs – seven-time Champions between 1959 and 1969 and twice Gillette Cup winners – became a famine during the 1970s. By then, the county had lost Fred Truman because of retirement and Close and Illingworth because the committee were a stroppy bunch far too full of themselves. Here were officials unable to understand that the status quo meant standing still, the start of Yorkshire's self-destruction. 'We were fools,' said Close, wincing at the wound the committee inflicted on him. 'Garry was a pal. He'd have fitted right in. But I was competing against history, and I lost. I couldn't persuade *anyone* that it was a good idea. The committee men just didn't see the sense in it. They wanted things to stay the same. One of them even said to me: "We don't need him. We've got all of Yorkshire to pick from." How bloody stupid was that? We were stuck in the era of Lord Hawke.' I remember Close shook his head and sucked deeply on one of the 20 or so cigarettes he smoked that morning and afternoon. He shook his head again and added: 'Think of the impact he'd have made. Think of the crowds. You'd have been laying on special buses for them. What a chance got wasted.' It would be another 20 years before Yorkshire, still suffering because of their own intransigence, at last hired a promising young fellow as their first overseas pro.

His name was Sachin Tendulkar.

With Dom Sibley gone, but fewer than 40 needed, you expect Warwickshire to gather in the rest of their runs without much disturbance. A frenzy grips them instead. Perhaps the job is just too simple. Four wickets fall in 62 balls – the last three of those in 32 deliveries. The most atrocious shot is an across-the-line haymaker, splattering Matt Lamb's stumps. When the score was 202 for four, Jeetan Patel was probably packing his pads away. On 215 for seven, he found himself walking out in them.

Should we ever doubt that some things are inexplicably meant to be? It is Patel, the player partly made in York, who clips the ball off his legs and sends it through mid-wicket to seal Warwickshire's victory. His 23-year-old self, seeing this ground for the first time, would never have believed that.

There are three Championship games I would like to have seen. The first, which is freakish, took place at Edgbaston in 1922 between Warwickshire and Hampshire. The headline in the *Birmingham Gazette* read 'THE UNEXPECTED HAPPENS'. This so blandly understates what did happen that the sub-editor who wrote it must have gone into a catatonic shock after absorbing the details. Anyone glancing at the scoreboard over breakfast will surely have assumed it was a collection of misprints. Hampshire, bowled out for 15 in 53 balls in their first innings, beat Warwickshire by 155 runs after piling up 521 in their second.

The second match is the one that brought Jack Hobbs his 126th century, drawing him level with W. G. Grace, at Taunton in 1925. Only one minute and 47 seconds of his innings survives on silent Pathé News film. You see Hobbs, aged 42, coming out of the dark pavilion, walking past men in stiff collars and straw boaters. He turns the ball off his pads and trots the crucial single. The modern cricketer would whoop and fist-pump the air. Hobbs raises his bat and doffs his cap, as if showing deference to a lady.

The third game was effectively the Championship decider of 1947, the summer in which the only thing not rationed in the country was sunshine. Denis Compton and Bill Edrich totalled almost 7,500 runs between them. Middlesex took the title, claiming it in all but name at Cheltenham where Gloucestershire, their nearest rivals, were beaten by 68 runs in a low-scoring contest on a dusty, spinner's pitch. 'Men still speak of the match,' wrote Frank Keating, who was a boy then, taking with him the sandwiches his mother had made for his lunch. 'You meet people in pubs who can recite Gloucestershire's second innings' scorecard. Only they don't weep at it any longer,' he added. I would give a lot to see what Keating saw: the boundary exploits of Clifford Monks. 'He sprinted, memory insists, some 50 yards to catch R. W. V Robins,' remembered Keating. 'Memory also insists that the ball would have hit me on the head had he not held it, but I've heard more than a dozen men claim that over the years. It remains the greatest catch I have ever seen.' When Monks died, in 1974, the *Cheltenham Echo* ran these words above his obituary: 'The Man Who Made the Catch'.

York won't inspire hosannas or spectacular headlines in the way that Edgbaston, Taunton or Cheltenham did.

The significance of the game lies in the link made with the past, giving us an affinity with it. You could tell this because, even though the result quickly became obvious, almost no one left Clifton Park; not even the ghosts of Bobby Peel and his aristocratic taskmaster.

Lord's: July 14, 2019: England celebrate after dramatically winning the World Cup against New Zealand.*

CHAPTER THREE

A Path through the Village

*A final framed in a single photograph. How cricket
became invisible. A Test Match on every Park. The mole-catcher
and the Lord. The superstar asks for middle and leg.
Kane Williamson goes unrecognised.*

You could still – almost, at least – hear the cheering. You could
still – without doubt – see the stir of images that had precip-
itated it. Only six days had gone by since England's World
Cup win over New Zealand on that Sunday of unsurpassed
tension at Lord's. You couldn't stop thinking about how a lost
cause was transformed into a triumph that had made cricket
instantly in vogue again. The term 'Super Over' had slipped
into the national vocabulary, becoming common usage for a
week.

The finale of the match was so inexpressibly fantastic that some spots on the old ground ought to have monuments built on them. The spot where Martin Guptill's throw ricocheted off the back of Ben Stokes's bat and ran away to the boundary beneath the press box, the outrageous fluke bringing England six runs when an accurate interpretation of the rules ought to have awarded them just five. The spot in front of the Grandstand where Jason Roy picked up Guptill's drive off Jofra Archer and chucked it towards the Pavilion End. The spot on which Jos Buttler gathered Roy's throw in front of the stumps and then flung himself at them. In our electronic age, the printed word gets dismissed as moribund or superfluous, but next morning – and the morning after that too – the dead-tree press spectacularly proved both claims to be a little exaggerated. Not stinting on ink and pagination, the newspapers offered us collectors' issues that demonstrated how the industry commemorates the great occasions far better than pixels on a phone or a computer screen ever can. *The Times*, for instance, produced a souvenir wraparound comprising a single photograph. The photograph freezes for us the final second of a story which had lasted eight hours and 49 minutes. The power in that picture lay not only in the decisiveness of the moment captured, but also in the symmetrical beauty contained within it. Even that most magnificent of portrait painters, Velázquez, couldn't have arranged the two figures to more sublime effect. Mostly we 'read' photographs in the same way that we read words – from left to right. This one needed to be read from right to left. On the extreme right is Buttler. His gloved left hand has broken the stumps, dislodging a bail. On the extreme left is Guptill, the player Fate chose to follow around all day. He is making a low, full-length dive for the crease, which is still two and a half yards from the toe of his dangling bat. The solid white line of that crease, the baked corn-colour of the pitch, the scuffed pale grass either side of it and the elongated shadow of Buttler's body accentuate the compositional impact of the shot. The angle at which the shutter closes on wicketkeeper and batsman is also so perfect – as though calibrated with mathematical instruments – that rapid motion is explicit in the still image.

We never saw coming the final we got because even the most ridiculously surreal imagination could not have scripted it. The implausibility of each new twist outdid the last until we finally learned to expect anything and rationalise everything, however unlikely or incredible it seemed.

The game came at us in a rush at the end. The 15 runs that England got off that 50th over to tie the scores on 251 . . . Ben Stokes, after his 84, and Buttler, after his half-century, banging another 15 between them in the Super Over that followed . . . Guptill, needing two, but getting only one before Buttler ran him out . . . the scores tied again . . . England winning on the basis of hitting more boundaries. Ever since, people who had previously shown no particular interest in cricket and know next to nothing about it have been discussing the game's finer points. Cricket has again become part of everyday conversation because of this match. For goodness' sake, you've been able to go into a pub or stand at a bus stop and hear debates about it. It's been like 2005, the epic Ashes summer that passed like a dream. Those of us then who were identified as established followers of the game were briefly able to wallow in being fashionable for the first time in our lives. We were sought out for our wisdom on Shane Warne's googly or the way in which Kevin Pietersen whacked the ball through mid-wicket on one leg. We quite liked it.

Cricket could have spent a billion on advertising and marketing without achieving the high profile or cultivating the goodwill that the 2005 series brought it. One company, Woodworm, sold 20,000 bats because Andrew Flintoff used one to flay the Australians. In less than three months, Flintoff sold more than 100,000 copies of the autobiography he subsequently published.

Shown live on terrestrial television, the series became a shared event. Afterwards, cricket had only to do the simplest thing to remain popular, which was to stay visible. Instead, the ECB took a decision that was financially lucrative but catastrophically stupid. The game was carried behind the paywall of satellite TV. The gamble assumed that enthusiasm alone would be sufficient to persuade all of us to follow it there. Alas, the business plan, based on raking in the loot, wasn't sophisticated enough to factor in how the poor live. Those who wanted to see more, but couldn't afford it, have never come back. The kindest thing you can say is that the

ECB zigged when it ought to have zagged. The less kind thing, but truer, is that it was just bloody greedy.

The ECB will shout back the claim that 2005 wasn't the seller's market we supposed it had been: the BBC was indifferent towards cricket and the other free-to-air broadcasters were apathetic. But – and this is the rub – it has had over ten years to work out a compromise; something that would enable cricket to get into the bloodstream and grab at the heart again, not just occasionally but regularly.

A generation was lost to cricket as soon as the game became invisible to them, which is why the renaissance didn't last. Every year the ECB has banked the big cheque, but that money can't buy the love and attention the sport needs to thrive. In 2008, there were 428,000 cricketers registered with clubs and village teams. By 2016, that figure had dipped to 278,000. Cricket in state education is as rare as Greek on the curriculum. If you don't play, you're unlikely ever to watch.

If I needed it (which I didn't), I had a bleak reminder about the difficulty of stoking up enthusiasm for cricket shortly after the season got under way. On Easter Saturday, I had walked to the seven-acre park that sits at the far end of my village. The sun was high and awfully hot. The short, lamp-black shadows it cast seemed to have some genuine depth; the eye almost tricked you into believing they were solid objects. The sky was practically unblemished. Just a few thin streaks of very white cloud hung across it. The weather was bespoke for a day at a County Championship match. I ought to have been at Trent Bridge, sitting in the Parr Stand. Or at Old Trafford, watching Jimmy Anderson pace out the 15 steps of his run with the new ball in his hand. Or especially somewhere on the coast, where the lightest of sea breezes would make the temperature bearable. But the fixture list is idiosyncratic, the rhyme and reason behind it often unfathomable. The ECB faffs about with it, usually for the benefit of Twenty20. Championship matches are now rarely staged on Saturdays. The focus is supposed to be on the grass-roots instead, which is a forlorn hope. And so that afternoon, which was beyond beautiful, was wasted. The nearest seriously competitive game was being staged in Rajasthan, where the Indian Premier League rolled on in a whirl of fours and sixes.

Bear with me. The worst is to come.

Our childhoods are with us for life. In mine, you could hardly move for magnificent Test matches fought out on the school field or on the nearby recreation ground, where the land rose and fell a little, creating undulations like humps of an infant camel. If you wanted to claim one of the prized 'pitches', you had to arrive early. We had a set of stumps that age had darkened, and we carried them in an old pad, the straps buckled tightly to stop them slipping out. We had an assortment of bats, some of them lacking their rubber grip and others badly cracked. The ball was cracked too and often ragged, as though a dog had chewed it like a bone. The seam was so flat that no one even expertly proficient in the darkest arts of ball tampering could have revived it. We also had a pair of wicketkeeper gloves so ancient that Herbert Strudwick could have owned them. The stench inside these gloves, from decades of accumulated sweat, was rancid. What we lacked was a decent pair of batting gloves. Sometimes your hands were badly bruised or cut; you looked as though you'd been in a bare-knuckle fight. We didn't care. We only wanted to play cricket. We played endlessly. From morning until lunch. From afternoon until late evening. We played until we were red raw from sunburn. We played in the rain. We played when the light was so poor that you could barely see the bowler's hand, let alone the ball after he released it; you pushed and prodded, surviving through gut instinct. I liked in particular those days when the corporation's machine, the size of a small combine harvester, mowed the grass and left the cuttings uncollected. Not only because it made the strip treacherously lively, the ball rising or jumping sideways, but also because the smell of the cut grass was intoxicating. These memories are on the one hand specifically personal and on the other common to anyone who has ever planted a set of stumps on a lush heath and pretended to be playing at Lord's.

On that Easter Saturday, I sat on a bench and looked around the park. Dogs were leaping about to catch skimmed frisbees. Boys were kicking a football between netless goalposts. An elderly couple were playing gentle tennis, lobbing shots at one another from the baseline. An enormous spread of ground was still redundant; only the odd walker strolled across it as a short cut to somewhere else. Conspicuous by its absence from this scene was cricket. In fact, I have *never* seen anyone play the game there.

Sky Sports charitably allowed the World Cup final to be screened live on Channel 4, the station which also showed the Ashes in 2005. Viewing figures for the match on both channels, according to the Broadcasting Audience Research Board, topped 8.7 million. On BBC, the Wimbledon final in which Djokovic thwarted the crowd favourite, Federer, drew an audience of 9.6 million.

Today, which is another sunny Saturday, the bizarreness of cricket's fixtures means that anyone galvanised by Stokes and Buttler and the glint of the World Cup trophy has few options to see a match. There are two Twenty20 games being played. One is at Chesterfield. The other is in Canterbury.

So I am taking the option that is easiest and most common for me. I am wandering the half-mile from my front door to the village cricket club. Menston's First XI are playing Calverley St Wilfrid's in Division Three of the Airedale & Wharfedale Senior Cricket League. On the way there, I will call in at the park again. In every analysis piece about the possible benefits of winning the white-ball World Cup has been the expectation that it will stimulate the red-ball game.

I want to see if that is happening in my own small corner of Yorkshire.

★

Time is a sneaky predator, stalking you almost surreptitiously until you look back and realise how many years have rolled by. When I last played village cricket, no one wore a helmet, which I knew even then wasn't entirely sensible. We put Blanco on our pads and linseed oil on our bats. The scorer sat beside a box of pencils. I played on pitches that were sometimes green enough to be indistinguishable from the outfield. A few of those outfields were either potholed, roughly overgrown or used during the week to graze a farmer's herd of cows, a fact which became particularly apparent if you had the misfortune to step in or slide across the evidence. Occasionally, we changed in the same concrete block where the groundsman stored the club mower behind padlocked double doors. There'd be a strong reek of petrol in the air. A fewer of the smaller, wooden dressing rooms had flat bitumen roofs, the wide strips of which became untacked because of age and blowy winds. The floors and walls could be damp. In the early part of the season, when you went into a match wearing at least two sweaters over a shirt and T-shirt, these places could also be colder than Captain Scott's hut. I never bothered about any of that. The summers I spent playing were some of the most companionable and hospitable of my entire life. I loved travelling along the narrow country lanes of the county in the cramped back seat of a car. I discovered villages I barely knew existed and I drank too much beer in their pubs. I was with friends who, like me, saw these Saturdays as an awfully big adventure for which we were hungry. We were young; just boys, really.

I would like to have played at The Fox ground in Menston.
The postcard view of it ought to be snapped from the top
corner, blocking out a three-storey block of flats that rises
alongside the railway. The line takes passengers as far as Ilkley
or to either Leeds or Bradford. You can look down on the
square, taking in the bushy trees, the long drystone wall that
runs beside the busy and frequently congested A65, the darker,
block-stone of the pavilion and also the bistro pub behind it.
The top of the field is ringed off by the sweep of a white picket
fence. The spire of a modern church stands in the middle
distance.

The club was formed in 1880, the year Gladstone beat
Disraeli in the General Election by at least six wickets. Menston's original ground, close by another pub and a different
church spire, was in the heart of the village. The club came
to The Fox seven years later, never shifting since. A shire horse
used to pull a stone roller along footpaths to prepare the pitch
and sheep spent the winter chewing on the outfield to keep
it trim. The pavilion had formerly been a farm house, lacking
both a toilet and electricity. Committee meetings were conducted in candlelight.

Like nearly every other village team then, and also for a
long while afterwards, Menston's was predominantly made
up of men who worked on and lived off the soil, the agricultural labourers and the farm hands. The local toff was
the captain, arriving in his whites to spare him the awk-
wardness of getting changed beside those whose wages he

paid and whose homes he owned. Everyone who writes about village cricket quotes G. M. Trevelyan because the historian had implacable opinions about it. In *English Social History*, first published in 1942, Trevelyan portrays the cricket field as the crucible of rural democracy. He goes as far as to argue that the French aristocracy could have dodged revolution if only some of them had played weekend cricket with the servants. I like the idea of the mole-catcher batting with the village Lord and bossing him about over whether to take that quick single; but, in truth, all men are equal only in the graveyard. The mole-catcher knew his place and tolerated it because he had no option; forelock-tugging was obligatory. I think Trevelyan overstated the friendship – if you can call it that – between them. I also think the importance of the village game lies elsewhere. We may no longer be able to define or definitively explain what England is – and coherently sum up the perfect place we want it to be – but we do know that it must include village cricket. Without it, the summer wouldn't be whole. As the distinctive feature of any village, it embodies character, community, old-fashioned customs and civility. Imagine it gone – and then imagine how you would feel.

I would be mortified.

To get to Menston's ground I have to go across the railway-station bridge and through an estate of houses built in the 1960s. I turn and walk down a ginnel, the ground visible only halfway along it. You hear the match going before you see it. Odd though this seems, the sight of the ground always comes as something of a surprise to me. It's as though I illogically expect someone to have moved or built over it in the week or two since I was last here.

It is the first weekend after July 16, a date significant only for those who remember this specific turn of the calendar once coincided with the village 'Feast'. A fair brought stalls and sideshows, rides and ornate caravans. The shining brass and whirling flywheels of giant steam engines stood on the field between the railway station and the pub. Alongside all the blare of that fair was a celebratory cricket match, often pitting Menston's President's XI against the Captain's XI.

Today it is pleasantly quiet, even drowsy. Calverley St Wilfrid's have won the toss, asking Menston to bat. There is the low hum of traffic on the road. Drinkers come out of The Fox with glasses on plastic trays and sit at the tables overlooking the field. I buy a pint and find a seat too.

Neville Ford of Middlesex once hit a six into a moving baby's pram. The baby slept on. Frank Woolley, at Kent, put a shot into a deckchair, which had just been abandoned by a 'very old woman'. Les Ames, also at Kent, knocked off a policeman's helmet. Always so close to the action in village cricket, you are ever vigilant against similar occurrences. The game here, however, begins with Menston losing three wickets and then a fourth for not many at all. The ball hardly comes near us.

★

One of the most eloquent descriptions about the small pleasures of cricket is so obscure that few know it even exists. The writer is obscure now too, undeservedly so, and the magazine in which his essay appeared curled up and died decades ago. I have been through shelves of anthologies in the hope of finding the article preserved in just one of them, which would let me throw away the tatty photocopy I own of it. It is never there.

Michael Meyer was a critic, playwright, novelist and translator. He also won a major literary prize for biography. Meyer originally wrote his piece as a talk for the BBC more than 70 years ago. It received such good reviews that the *Listener*, which the corporation published weekly, printed it over two pages. Within them, evident in every paragraph, beats the true and besotted heart of a cricket man. Meyer asks: 'I wonder what this peculiar appeal of cricket is; what is it that makes Englishmen sit for hours watching the slow game . . . Why on earth do we do it? Why do we watch cricket?' The questions are a tease, pulling us like a line of rope towards the answers Meyer has long known. He holds back for a while, only so he can hang other observations on to them. Even in highlighting the hardships of the spectator – 'at least a third of the day's play is always pretty dull', he insists – Meyer is like the mountaineer who deliberately accentuates the difficulty of the climb so the view from the summit is more spectacular.

He starts with the 'minor reasons' for cricket's allure. One of these is: 'It's always fun to watch other people exerting themselves – that's why we look at men mending the road or lugging a piano through somebody's front door.' The second is that 'there is something mystical and impressive' about the sight of a cricket match. A third, which is connected to the second, is that cricket counts as a 'fine landscape painter' and cricket grounds are 'almost always pleasant spots', which 'isn't always true of places where they play other games'.

Meyer was particularly attracted to the village game. To play it, he said, was one of the most noble 'occupations any man can turn to'. He ranked it as being 'serious without being a matter of life and death'. The greens on which games were staged captivated him too. Each had its own 'individual flavour', he explained, because 'they have generally grown out of the countryside and buildings have grown up around them. They have often not been imposed on a landscape.'

To press home this last point, the *Listener* chose a very pastoral photograph to illustrate Meyer's thoughts. It shows a game on the common at Frenchay in South Gloucestershire. Spectators picnic on blankets laid across the scrubby, slightly long grass on the apron of the boundary. The odd bicycle lies beside them. There is an assortment of trees: beech and maple, oak and elm. The spire of St John the Baptist church, majestic next to the sight screen, is as slender as a bodkin. The only thing missing from the scene is a friendly dog or two.

Meyer is right. Village cricket is gravely 'serious' for those who play it. For those of us who watch, however, the atmosphere, rather than the competition, is what counts. Often unaware of how the game is progressing, we tend to glance at the scoreboard only when a wicket is taken or a flurry of boundaries is struck. So we recognise rather slowly that Calverley St Wilfrid's, relegated last season but pushing for immediate promotion, are beginning to find the hosts more of a struggle than initially anticipated. Their early success isn't leading to a rout. In May, Calverley beat Menston by 106 runs. That sort of shellacking will not be repeated.

Menston's 'overseas' player is the twenty-nine year-old all-rounder Thiroshin Naidoo, a South African. His captain, Adam Montague-Millar, also the wicketkeeper, joins him in a flourishing middle-order partnership.

Meyer thought 'cricket has a much stronger sense of comedy than other games'. He was right. More than anyone else, I think, the average village cricketer has a style distinctively his own. I have actually seen one bowler who could have sprung out of P. G. Wodehouse. Before delivering the ball, he did take 'two short steps, two long steps, gave a jump, took three more short steps and ended with a step and jump'. I have seen a batsman take guard outside leg, utterly surprised when his off stump suddenly wasn't there any more. I have seen every possible form of dismissal too – even 'handling the ball' and 'timed out' (a tail-ender went to the shops, thinking his presence was no longer required).

Nothing in Menston versus Calverley is as unorthodox as

any of that, but it nevertheless soon reminds me of almost every other village match I have ever seen. There are wides and byes and no balls. There are thickish edges and catches that ought to be taken but are put down. The ball goes missing for five minutes in a hedge. There is also a marvellously meaty drive from Naidoo, the back lift generous and the shot so very clean that it imitates a little the exploits of Stokes and Buttler at Lord's.

Naidoo was signed after Menston's Head of Senior Cricket heard about his abilities from contacts in Durban. He'd been playing for Delta CC, who are based in Overport. Even in the chilliest months there, the temperature can reach 25 degrees. When Naidoo unpacked and began practising here last spring – he had never seen England before – it was a fairly balmy week only insofar as you no longer required an overcoat; Naidoo was 'cold'. Today it is so genuinely warm that winter's hard heart has properly melted. He feels at home, going on to make 61. Montague-Millar is three short of his half-century. Whether Menston can defend their total of 156, which is a little below par, probably depends on Naidoo too; he will take the new ball.

Somehow, for reasons unfathomable now, I spent a season on the General Purposes Committee of my old village club. I learned that, like Tolstoy's happy families, they are 'all alike', not only in their collection of disparate characters –

the shyly unassuming, the nervy, the egotistically bossy who likes to inflate his own talent, the fusspots and those sanguinely indifferent – but also in the difficulties facing them. Our budget was always tight because our funds were always scarce. You were constantly chivvying some members into paying their subscription or their match fee. Often, I thought, we were like the housewife who could afford bread but not the butter to put on it. Jam was a fantasy. The fabric of the club had to be kept in constant repair. We relied on volunteer labour and spirit, the odd donation and acts of benevolence. From buying tins of paint to printing fixture cards, everything was a slog.

Every so often a coffee-table book of photographs depicting chocolate-box grounds will appear. You fall into it knowing what you'll find: broad trees or soft hills; a black square scoreboard or a mock Tudor pavilion; the view through a weathered lychgate; the sight of a couple of spectators sitting on a boundary bench; a long trestle table set for tea, the cake and the cut sandwiches already laid out; a dressing room where a well-used bat rests against a wall near a window, the afternoon light dropping diagonally across the splice. I buy these books, finding them irresistible, but I can't look at the bucolic scenes without thinking that some poor bugger runs his arse off every year to make sure Eden survives and looks like that.

The hackneyed phrase 'stalwart servant' sticks to Paul Smith, the chairman and secretary of Menston. He joined them around 25 years ago as a junior. He is spot on with figures. He can tell you about the minutiae of the accounts and the membership, which is about 200, and the club's history year by year. What Smith refuses to tot up are the number of hours he devotes to his club. 'I don't like to go there,' he says. His son plays for the under-15s. His 11-year-old daughter turns out for the girls' team. Mrs Smith pitches in with the teas.

Smith became chairman at the beginning of a decade that has seen the ground smartened up and improved. 'There's still some way to go,' he insists.

The land belongs to the owners of the pub, the lease agreed as far back as 1940. It is inconceivable that the landlord would evict his tenant and risk the opprobrium of the village, which would rise up in a pitchfork protest. So the pavilion was extended, courtesy of an interest-free loan from the ECB. The practice facilities are about to become plusher because of a grant from Sport England. The next task is patching up the pavilion roof. 'It's bowing and some tiles are missing,' explains Smith. Menston are always thinking about the next raffle, the next Fun Day, Golf Day or Band Night that will claw some cash into the club. 'Sometimes it feels like we need to do it just to stand still,' says Smith.

It has always been like this. The author of a book commemorating Menston's centenary in 1980 made a prediction of imminent doom characteristic of the most gloomy Roman oracle. 'The economic climate of our time makes survival more and more difficult,' he wrote. 'Next season the umpires for a match will cost as much as £10' [and] a cricket ball will soon cost £20'. He concluded that 'sooner or later' many clubs 'will face insolvency – particularly those like Menston without the proceeds of a licensed bar'. In 2019, umpires cost up to £100 per game. A ball is £25, the price held down because manufacturing became quicker and cheaper. The club now benefits from its own bar too. The income gleaned from it is precious. The annual sum required to run the club will still astonish anyone who considers village cricket to be the inexpensive and casual hobby of a few flannelled fellows who do nothing more than stroll up and play every weekend. Phenomenal effort is necessary simply to exist.

Menston's lease is £300. Utilities, such as electricity and water, are £1,200. There is also insurance (£1,500), licences (£600) and fees (another £600) to the Airedale & Wharfedale League(s). The upkeep of the playing area – Menston prides itself on that – is £10,000. Other assorted bills include teas (£2,000 plus), scorers (more than £1,200), indoor nets and coaching courses (not far off £6,000). Even bar expenses top £7,000.

Total costs are about £50,000.

'It's the way of things,' Smith explains stoically. 'You have to ensure the club is still here for the next generation. That's the job.'

Cash isn't Menston's only concern. At the last census, the village's population was two residents shy of 4,500. There isn't a lot of doorstep talent on which to draw. The club, like every other, competes with the everyday demands of family and social life. Smith has calculated that on average Menston's first XI players are only available once every two weeks. Second XI players are only available once every four. In 2017, the Second XI won promotion. Just two of them still play regularly.

You would hardly credit that Menston, small as it is, once had two top-drawer names on the team sheet. The village has a literary claim to fame; Eric Knight, who wrote *Lassie*, was born here. He doesn't outshine for me the two cricketers, luminous in Menston's history. The first is the gangly, bespectacled Bill Bowes. A road named after him is a five-minute saunter from the ground.

Wisden said Bowes resembled 'a university professor' and concluded 'there has probably never been a great cricketer who looked less like one'. It was Bowes who bowled Donald Bradman for a first ball duck during the Bodyline series. He silenced the MCG to the extent that the only sound heard on Bradman's lonely walk back to the dressing room was the rattle of Melbourne's trams. With Yorkshire, he won seven County Championship titles before the Second World War. Bowes played for Menston in the summer it ended. He served in North Africa and got captured there, shedding four stones in prison camps before his release.

Geography has given me a special interest in Bowes. From my kitchen window I can see the red-tiled roof of the house he lived in, the chequered greenery of the Wharfe Valley spreading beyond what used to be his back garden fence. I imagine one day catching sight of him, between the trees, as he walks along the lane that bends between his home and mine. John Arlott regularly stayed with Bowes when he came to Yorkshire. The two of them would regularly be found in the Menston Arms, the pub nearest to Bowes's home. Arlott always signed and sent him every book he wrote on the game. When, a few years ago, a bookseller's catalogue advertised some of those titles, I felt it right and proper to buy a couple, bringing them back to the village.

Bowes made his debut for Menston on Whit Monday, 1945: 'What an attraction he created', said one account, '. . . like a man with two heads.' There is a photograph of Bowes walking on to the field that day. He is in a thick sweater, the knitted, broad V of it stretching from one shoulder blade to the other. There is another photograph of those who crammed into the ground to watch him. Men in trilbys or cloth caps sit on or lean against the drystone wall protecting the ground from the main road. The angle the photographer chose allows you to look up that road and spy on those who are walking or cycling down it and also two cars, which have just passed one another on an otherwise empty highway.

Bowes didn't disappoint his audience. He took his first wicket in his third over and soon claimed another six, finishing with figures of seven for 17. North Leeds, only there to be whipped, were 45 all out. That season, Bowes bowled

1,260 balls for Menston and claimed 72 wickets at eight apiece; he averaged a wicket every three overs. That statistic could have been more impressive still. His most vivid memory was of a substitute fielder who in one match folded his arms at mid-off and refused to take two dolly catches. When asked why, the fielder told Bowes tartly that a bowler of his pedigree shouldn't have to rely on catches. 'You can bowl 'em out,' he said.

The second player is Martin Crowe.

Elegant and explosively stylish, a purist possessing classical technique, Crowe almost qualified as an honorary York-shireman. He lacked only the flat cap, the white muffler and a whippet and a pint of Timothy Taylor. He had already played for Bradford and Pudsey St Lawrence. He had toiled in the nets at Headingley too, bowling to Geoffrey Boycott but seldom batting himself; Boycott was reluctant to give him a turn, it seems. Crowe made his first-class debut at seventeen and took his Test bow at nineteen. He was two months short of his 24th birthday when Menston recruited him mid-season in 1985. The previous April in Guyana, during New Zealand's Test series against the West Indies, he took 188 off an attack that included Malcolm Marshall, Michael Holding and Joel Garner. His match-saving innings on a flattish pitch lasted nine and a half hours. In that same month *Wisden* garlanded him as one of its Cricketers of the Year.

Signing Crowe was the equivalent today of Menston's Amateur Dramatic Society getting his Oscar-winning first cousin, Russell, to play the lead role in the *Pirates of Penzance* and then staging the musical in the Community Centre next to the library.

In 1984 Crowe had replaced Viv Richards at Somerset, a job so onerous that even his best might not have been good enough. He initially lived with Ian Botham. After five successive single-figure scores, he decided to seek alternative accommodation. He broached the sensitive matter with Botham when his house-mate was soaking in the bath. As Vic Marks reported, 'there wasn't much he (Botham) could do about it from there'. By the end of the summer, Crowe had scored over 1,700 runs.

After Richards's return to Taunton the following summer – and Garner's too – Crowe found himself as the spare part. He was eligible to play for Somerset only if both of them didn't. He was travelling from New Zealand to Yorkshire for a two month break; he planned to do nothing more than catch up with a few old friends and play occasionally for Somerset's Second XI. Menston's hierarchy knew someone who knew him. Crowe came to the village because he was asked and also because Menston, then bottom of the table, were perceptive enough to recognise a rare chance before grasping it. Crowe arrived with factory-fresh bats, courtesy of his sponsor, and blew into the car park before one match as a passenger in the sort of Mustang that Steve McQueen drove in *Bullitt*.

You'll find his contribution to the Airedale & Wharfedale

Senior Cricket League in the West Yorkshire Archives, where Menston sent their original scorebooks. In seven appearances, he made 355 runs at an average of just over 67. His big scores were 82 against Burley, 76 against Adel and an unbeaten 66 against Addingham. Only Otley, the first team Crowe faced, got away lightly against him. Still sleeping off his jet-lag, he lasted only eight minutes and 12 balls, making a couple of singles.

Crowe's contribution to that summer was rated 'the finest exhibition of batting and fielding ever likely to be seen in local cricket'. He had company. Menston also hired another New Zealander, Derek Stirling, a brisk medium-pace bowler who was a rapid runmaker too. Once, Stirling is said to have lit a cigarette, taken a drag on his way out to bat and then left it to burn on the pavilion fence. He hit 90 at such a rate that, after being dismissed, he finished the same cigarette on his way back to the dressing room. The story is so good that I concede the absolute implausibility of it only with enormous reluctance.

Of course, Crowe was the star performer. He would go on to play 77 Tests, making nearly 5,500 runs. The League, far from singing hallelujahs after he turned up and took guard on middle and leg, went into a little huff afterwards. It was peeved that 'the Press' had learnt of Crowe's signing before them. Menston were told the league's management committee would be reviewing the 'wording and workings' of the rule that governed overseas signings. This, it did. No one of Crowe's status has ever been seen again on the fields of Airedale and Wharfedale.

Oddly, his cameo at Menston, as fleeting as a holiday romance, wasn't mentioned in either of his autobiographies. The club nevertheless have not forgotten him or what he achieved for them. Crowe was the superhero who came to their rescue. The team finished ninth, side-stepping relegation.

Thiroshin Naidoo doesn't bowl like Bill Bowes or bat like Martin Crowe. The runs he made are nevertheless complemented in late afternoon with wickets. He takes three for 13 from just six overs, an analysis marred only by the fact he bowled seven wides. Calverley never stand a chance. At one stage, they are 17 for four, their first five batsmen making only ten between them. Calverley do rally, but are bowled out for 140 – 16 short – in only 31.4 overs.

One thought always gnaws away at me while watching Menston. I ought, like the 70-year-old I met at York, to still be playing somewhere for someone. I see a delivery that scoots through a wicketkeeper's legs. I see a leg-spinner lose his grip on the ball, which floats like a balloon towards mid-wicket. I see a batsman pat down a delivery that should be driven straight back. Or he swings across the line, his stumps spread like skittles in an alley. I'd have snapped up the ball the wicketkeeper let through for byes. I'd have bowled my leg-spinner on a length. I'd have sent that delivery for four – at least – and then blown on the toe of my bat the way a Western gunfighter blows on the muzzle of his revolver. It's nonsense, of course.

We feed the heart on fantasies. The minuscule talent I once possessed fled and refused to return. Any comeback I made might last only one ball.

I used to go to winter coaching, first at Nottinghamshire and then (after a minor difference of opinion) at Leicestershire. I wanted to be a County Championship cricketer more than anything else on God's earth. At Grace Road, we were hemmed into nets that would have troubled the claustrophobic. The coach was Ray Julian, an immensely patient instructor. I have to say that I gave up on myself shortly before he rightly gave up on me. One Saturday morning, I glanced into the far net and saw someone so conspicuously better than all of us. Time seemed to bend to his will. The sound of his strokes off the middle was like singing. 'Who's that?' I asked, not having seen this figure before. 'Don't worry,' came the reply. 'He's older than us. And he's only here for a knock up.'

It was David Gower.

If I'd known then what Gower would go on to achieve, I'd have been far less depressed about my own inadequacies. I knew the game was up as far as a career was concerned. I was keen, nonetheless, to go on playing for the pure enjoyment of it; even a disorganised game on scrubland would do.

Those matches appear generally to be a thing of the past. No one is playing on the park in Menston on the afternoon when Calverley are beaten. The World Cup and the Super Over could have occurred a year ago rather than the previous weekend.

It makes me think of Kane Williamson.

When that final is played and replayed on TV, as it endlessly will be, I hope everyone remembers Williamson, who demonstrated such dignity in defeat. He was so humbly becoming and generous that the founder members of the Corinthians were probably applauding him. He knew New Zealand ought to have won the match. He knew also that something unprecedented and quite ridiculous had denied them. He could have sulked or been obstreperously moody, offering profound disappointment as mitigation afterwards. The graciousness in him just came out naturally instead. Who else would have responded to New Zealand's catalogue of bad luck and calamities with the line: 'One of those things, eh?'

Listening to him say it made me realise how much cricket those without Sky Sports subscriptions had actually missed.

I remembered going to the O2 store in Leeds to sort out some trifling matter with my phone. I explained to the sales assistant that I was a bit pressed for time; I was on my way to Headingley for a Championship match. 'We had a guy in here last week,' the assistant said, cheerfully. 'He was a cricketer. I thought he just played in one of the local leagues at the weekend. It turns out he's in the Yorkshire team, I think.' I asked the assistant the name of his customer. 'Kane somebody or other,' he said. 'He seemed a really decent bloke.'

This was the summer of 2014. Yorkshire won the Championship and Williamson made over 600 runs in nine games for them at an average of 57.18. His highest score was 189, accumulated in eight hours during the Scarborough Festival.

I told the sales assistant that the 'really decent bloke' was one of the world's premier batsmen. 'Is he? Blimey, I didn't have a clue,' he replied. The sales assistant, it ought to be stressed, also assumed Williamson was Australian. I told him about the artistic dignity and comportment Williamson displayed at the crease. I then told him how easily he made scoring runs seem, boiling down the components of batting to the classy essentials. As Mark Nicholas pointed out so perceptively: 'He bats with the voice of reason in his head, an uncomplicated man going about a complicated task unusually well . . . If a ball is pitched up, Williamson moves forward. If a ball is short, he plays back.' I gabbled on until I noticed the sales assistant's eyes had gone glassy. It was as if I had taken a cloth soaked in chloroform and held it against his face.

That short exchange emphasised for me cricket's difficulty in establishing itself in the consciousness of a public who are no longer used to seeing it. When even high-calibre talent such as Williamson goes unrecognised, the game surely has to consider how pitifully it has sold itself in the past 14 years.

My friends and I were inspired by what we saw on that small box in the living room. TVs back then were usually black and white, a 16-inch screen the norm and the quality of the picture – often shadowy or hazy – depended on the weather and robustness of your aerial. But you could watch every summer Test, the Gillette Cup and the John Player League and even – if you were close enough to the right transmitter – the Roses matches.

The BBC, which once cared about the game, used to produce a paperback book called *Armchair Cricket*. It was primarily aimed at the relative newcomer rather than the connoisseur. In the 1975 edition, there is a chapter called Television Production. The content is enlightening because it makes the coverage we got seem like something from the early days of Reith. There were only ever four cameras on the ground. The master camera was placed at one end. The second camera was beside it, employed just for wide shots. The third and fourth cameras were stuck at deep square leg and either at mid-on or mid-off. There were no fancy graphics (not long before, the score was flashed up in copperplate on handwritten white card). There was no stump microphone. There was no Spidercam. Even the slow-motion machine, the BBC advised, should be used sparingly and 'with care, particularly if it tends to throw doubt on umpires' decisions'. Today, because of Sky Sports, no Test is televised without at least 40 cameras. A player can't pick his nose or scratch his backside without being noticed. As for roughing up the ball . . . well, you'd have to be a blockhead, completely doolally or an Australian to try it.

The coverage, however exceptional and infinitesimally detailed in every regard, is nonetheless only of value if everyone can watch it.

Until that happens, the field in my village will remain empty of small cricket matches and one of the best runmakers in the present game will still be 'Kane somebody or other' to that sales assistant in the mobile-phone store.

First ball, first wicket. Sam Robson gets a feathery edge
against Ollie Robinson at Hove

CHAPTER FOUR

The Sea, the Sea

The bookseller as clairvoyant. The china cup and
the pot-mug. A place of quiet beauty. The bowler chasing
Verity and Laker. The telegraph boy at the pavilion gate.
Four quarters of blue cloth.

There are certain routes I always take to particular grounds. I regard each as bespoke to that place.

In Nottingham, for instance, I walk across Trent Bridge, the sprawl of the city at my back, and look down on the strangely still river. I trace the bend of it, picking out the pleasure boats, the athletic rowers and also the swans, gleaming snow-white against the black water. It reminds me of my boyhood here. In Manchester, I stroll down Warwick Road in honour of Neville Cardus, who went this way to Old Trafford

– originally as a ragamuffin with sixpence in his pocket and later during his Golden Age, between the wars, when no one writing about the game was more eagerly read. In London, NW8, I set off for the Grace Gates from the Georgian brick of Dorset Square, the first site Thomas Lord claimed as his own to make some 'brass' out of cricket. I turn right at the bottom end of Lisson Grove – where the Yorkshire entrepreneur shrewdly decamped to mow and roll his second field – and turn sharply right again at the top of it, a half-mile journey best enjoyed in a lazy, quarter-of-an-hour amble. There are benefits to this. The shape of Lord's, hidden until then, rises so suddenly along the St John's Wood Road that I always imagine the sight of its steep stands astonishes anyone who isn't expecting to find them there.

Today, an August Sunday, I am on another of my preferred but slightly quirky paths to a match. I am heading to the County Ground at Hove for the game between Sussex and Middlesex. My starting point is near Brighton's Palace Pier, the wide boards of which have stretched into the Channel since 1899, the year that K. S. Ranjitsinhji, the jewel in Sussex's batting, achieved what no one had before. He made more than 3,000 runs in a season, doing so in the immaculate style that mattered to him.

I never come to Hove without thinking of the old boy and the photograph George Beldam took of him. Bat aloft, like a lethal weapon, Ranji is not so much dancing out of his crease as going on a maniacal war charge, his left leg intimidatingly high, as though there is a hurdle to be straddled before he can meet the ball. Ranji was a curious sort of chap. Severely self-critical, he once dismissed a 'well played, sir' with an observation that comes across as a mild rebuke to the dunderhead who made it: 'No, I did not play well. Look at my pads. They are not clean.' Some minor misjudgments had left behind telltale blemishes of red dye, a sign of inadequacy to the perfectionist.

Ranji epitomises the spirit of Sussex, and also the ambitious showman's panache that I forever associate with the way it plays. His successors were Ted Dexter and Tony Greig, Imran Khan and Nawab of Pataudi, who would wander through the pavilion gate as though the Championship was a garden party. I have such an endearing regard for Sussex because of them all – and also because that striving to be simultaneously expressive, elegant and entertaining is innate in the county's cricket. The nature of the coast is responsible for that, I think. Temperament is nurtured in landscape, a fact that explains the breeziness in Sussex's character.

The atmosphere of cricket by the sea is always different from cricket anywhere else. But cricket at Hove is different again because Sussex are rooted in it rather than coming here like holidaymakers, unpacking their kit for the odd game and arriving home before the postcards. Go back a generation or so and you'll find that the County Championship fixtures used to dispatch Essex to Southend, Kent to Folkestone or Margate, Somerset to Weston-super-Mare, Hampshire to

Bournemouth and Lancashire to Lytham St Annes. Nottinghamshire flirted for a while with Cleethorpes. Sussex would
temporarily abandon Hove to stage Championship games at
both Eastbourne and Hastings, the latter so long buried
beneath concrete that archaeologists would need drills and
jackhammers before combing for fragments of it. This season,
Glamorgan have been to Colwyn Bay. Yorkshire, as always,
made a beloved home away from home at Scarborough, where
as many as 5,000 and more often squeeze through the narrow
turnstiles. The demise of the first-class match by the seaside
is demonstrated by the lack of any others. Most resorts that
once hosted one – and put out flags in gratitude – are like
neglected railway stations from the age of Beeching, rarely
used or entirely abandoned. Those of us, like me, who were
fortunate enough to have been born beside the sea never miss
the chance to return. We know the sight and swell of it, which
is ever-changing, will hold our gaze like a hypnotist's watch
and chain. We know we'll find the air sharper, cleaner and
fresher; we'll take gulps of it in like water. We know the sky
will be wider, higher and far fuller than it is inland and also
that the hard edge of the horizon, appearing like a faraway
country, will create the illusion of almost infinite space.

That is why I am at Hove. That is also why, earlier in the
season, I made my annual pilgrimage to Scarborough to sit
on the benches of the Popular Bank. Yorkshire were facing
the champions Surrey, unable to defend their title with anything but the limpest of fists. Of course, I have a specific

route to that ground too, a small map of my own making through the streets. I head off from the leafy Crescent, where the art gallery is hidden away, and cut more or less diagonally across the town. What I most like about Scarborough is how much of it stays the same from one summer to the next. Amid the constant chop and churn of everything else in this world, it is reassuring to go back and find things there almost exactly as I left them months or even a year before. The cafés cooking all-day breakfasts, serving tea so strong that you could creosote a fence with it. The funicular railway. The open-topped bus rocking along the North Bay. The donkeys being led sedately across the sands. The boarding houses with their paved front gardens, packed with terracotta pots of geraniums and begonias. The railway-station clock, the hands of which seem to have been stuck at five past two for a decade. The hotel where Wilfred Owen occupied a lonely tower and wrote some of his final poetry before being shipped back to the Front. There is a blousy side to Scarborough as well. A vape shop isn't coy about proclaiming pedigree and significance, as if it is already worthy of English Heritage status: 'Proudly Helping the Smokers of Scarborough since 2008', it says. At the ground itself, right in front of the gates, is an old-fashioned signpost, the sort you would find on a rural road, emphasising North Marine Road's individuality. One arm points towards Lord's, measuring it as 190 miles away. The subliminal message is a cheeky one: you are emphatically 'oop north'.

In the pavilion you'll find photographs, some of them snapped a century ago, that you think could almost be contemporary because so little change has taken place. The changes you do detect have been done with a kindly and sympathetic hand, seldom disturbing history. Lord Hawke has been dead for eighty-odd years, but he would immediately recognise North Marine Road if he climbed out of his grave in Lambeth and came here again.

Scarborough is a solid pot-mug compared to Hove's china cup and saucer. These two spots are nevertheless integral to the Championship. I cannot imagine the competition without them.

The palette of the coast is usually so vivid: the wooden deck-chairs, striped white and blue; the vermilion awnings that shadow al-fresco dining; the neon signage, chrome yellow and even fandango pink, illuminating the amusement arcades; the brightly painted frontages of trinket and novelty shops or the ice-cream parlours and rock emporiums. Then there is the scent of the seaside. The waft of salt and brine, fish and chips and the tang of vinegar, candy floss and toffee apples. But with split-second punctuality of the unfortunate kind, I arrived this morning with the first spit of rain, which soon became a steady drizzle. Thickly banked clouds shut out every peep of the sun and leeched the colour away, giving a monochrome tint to the seafront. The pebbly beach was empty.

The cafés were empty too, their plastic seats turned upside down to keep them dry. The Channel was flat and sickly looking, the frothy waves uninviting. A gusty breeze, coming in from the east, blew cold, damp air into my face. With the covers on, and the outfield already so richly green that it resembled the soft baize of a snooker table, Hove looked forlorn and bedraggled. I was browsing the second-hand bookstall when the rain became so hard that it drummed loudly off the low roof for ten gloomy minutes. Shallow puddles formed in hollows across the concourse. Surface water glistened near the boundary rope in front of the South Stand. Drips fell from the lid and the lip of the pavilion. The bookseller, a fixed point of the summer here, seemed unconcerned by this. He reassured the pessimists among us (especially me), telling us not to fret. The day would *not* be a washout, he said. I watched the bookseller stick out his hand, rain splashing on to his palm, and then tilt his gaze heavenwards, as if he was able to divine the weather to come purely from the nap of the clouds and the slivers of pale sky visible between them. 'Play will start at 2.30 p.m.,' he announced. It sounded like the rashest of promises, until the gush of rain stopped as abruptly as it had started. Within another ten minutes, the wind, which had dragged the cloud towards us like an enemy, performed the friendly gesture of dragging it away again. The sky became spotless.

In the beginning I'd had no choice but to come directly to the ground to avoid a small soaking. I felt out of joint. Now

I could go into Brighton, saunter about and come back again, dropping down on to the shoreline. The whole resort, maudlin and inanimate before, came alive at last. I saw familiar landmarks: the Old Ship Hotel, the Grand Hotel, the black-boned skeleton of the West Pier, which fire devoured and also Embassy Court, the modernist design of its eleven floors making the building look like an ocean liner about to set sail for France; I daydream about living in one of those flats, the cricket so close that I could go for the morning session and come home for lunch.

The turn on to First Avenue, which runs into Selborne Road, constitutes the last leg of the trek. Here are tall houses with wrought-iron fences and balconies and also big, heavy trees; their roots have cracked the pavement and lifted up paving slabs, a minor earthquake of Nature. There is a blue plaque commemorating the boyhood home of Patrick Hamilton (sadly, no relation), the neglected novelist who, along with Graham Greene, made Brighton seedy and sinister and attractively raffish for me.

August is the month in which I am always aware of the summer going on ahead of us, running out far too fast. Even an hour's rain robs something valuable from those special days. But outside the church of St John the Baptist, decorated by flint and stone, the flower-stall displays sunflowers with heads the size of lunch plates, a reminder that we have to grasp at August as it flies, catching whatever we can of it. As if to endorse that, I am standing among a gaggle of other spectators at the main gate, when a tannoy announcement is made. 'The umpires have decided that play will commence at 2.30 p.m.' We rush inside, desperate not to miss a ball.

I am in awe of the bookseller, a clairvoyant.

A short passage from Henry James, who lived along the coast at Rye, never fails to carry me back to all the cricket and the cricketers I have ever seen. It is this: 'Summer afternoon, summer afternoon; to me those have always been the two most beautiful words in the English language.'

James wasn't referring to the game, but the semi-colon is so exquisitely placed that the pause it creates, no more than a half-breath, allows you to attach whatever context you like to the sentiment. You see a roll of images entirely of your memory's making, the past slotting together into the present like a dovetail joint. But on this summer afternoon, I am waiting for another sentence, which is less poetic but just as evocative as James's:

'And from The Sea End . . . '

Those five words evoke Hove as a place of quiet beauty for me – even if I am a hundred or more miles away from it when I hear them. I see the hospitality tents, the low blocks of flats, which wrap themselves around the ground, the small, tucked-away scoreboard and the cramped stripes of the field. Looking down on that scene from one of the high rows of the South Stand, I identify Hove's limitations – it is a quaint ground rather than a grand one – but accept them as quirks.

I hope the first over will be bowled from The Sea End rather than The Cromwell Road End. Sussex, however, delay me that small pleasure after putting Middlesex in. Not far from a piled heap of sawdust, Ollie Robinson is pacing out his downhill gallop while Sam Robson taps at the pitch suspiciously, as if slightly fearful of what he might find there after all the rain. He takes guard and then steps out of his crease to poke around again, more tentatively than before.

A delayed start almost always means the opening exchanges are an anticlimax, the match taking a little while to get even into middle gear. Not today. People are still arriving, finding a seat or settling into one. Some are fumbling in bags or unfolding newspapers and so miss the first ball, which Robinson pitches well up and moves minimally away. That smidgen of late swing is enough to condemn Robson. His feet, which did so much wandering about before, are rigid on the crease. The ball takes the outside edge, the snick audible. It is straightforward catching practice for the wicketkeeper, Ben Brown. Aghast at misreading that delivery, and then not yanking the bat safely away, Robson departs briskly and with his head down, the walk back a tortuous embarrassment.

I keep a commonplace book, recording the things I overhear at cricket matches. So at Scarborough, I eagerly wrote down the story one man told his friend about his impatient response to some wretchedly slow scoring at Headingley. He detailed the slashing criticism he made of the batsman responsible for it, the content of which requires censoring to protect the sensitive among us. Suffice to say, he blasted invective at him for an hour and a quarter, barely noticing the woman sitting silently in front of him, her shoulders slowly hunching. She finally swivelled around and let loose with some slashing criticism of her own. Her language was Prussian blue. She was the batsman's wife.

At Hove, there is a cricketing novice, a woman in her 30s, who finds the rigmarole of the game profoundly cryptic. 'What are those men waiting for?' she asks, pointing at the slips. When Robson is out, she doesn't appreciate the rarity of the moment she has witnessed or understand the fact that a mistake, rather than a misfortune, led to it. She expresses maternal sympathy for Robson, her voice crackling with concern and pity. 'Oh,' she begins, her lament so solemn that it almost becomes lachrymose. 'It's so, so unfair. He must be *really* upset. He's waited so long to come in. Can't they give him another go?'

The Test sweater and cap that Robson owns make him a bold name on the scorecard. But with a few others to come – Nick Gubbins and Dawid Malan among them – his vanishing is considered to be a blip. No one foresees the messy collapse of Middlesex's top and middle order that Robinson is about to single-handedly initiate.

David Wiese claims The Sea End. With his arrival, I tot up all the other bowlers I have seen perform here: John Snow (with his loping run), Imran Khan (who, like Robinson, preferred the top end), Garth Le Roux, Chris Jordan et al. I add

Wiese's name to the list, his fast medium solid but mundane. He is never much of a nuisance to Middlesex. He is more an irritant to those of us soon willing Robinson on. We only want to watch him bowl – from both ends if possible.

Knowing conditions are beneficial for them, there are bowlers who overstretch, snatching at the bounty on offer and failing to grasp it as a consequence. Robinson is savvy. He is a man in charge of his circumstances. He becomes magnificently productive by making sure he adheres to the basics, the bedfellows of length and line. He lets the ball do the hard graft for him. He is neither particularly brawny nor mean-looking, which can easily fool the unwary. But he bowls stump to stump and with a Pythagorean exactitude. On this day, and at this hour, his right hand is so firm and so steady, and his eye so accurate, that I am sure he could take a pencil and draw a perfect circle – a task impossible for all but great artists. His pace is nothing racy either: about 84–6 mph, which is hardly a roar of fire. Those full deliveries kiss the top of the pitch instead and wobble either way, the direction of them hard to read. Nor does he rush around. On the way back to his mark, he pauses ruminatively. He digs his spikes into the turf or runs his fingers through his short blond hair. As he's about to turn, he'll either stroke the stubble on his chin, the bristles so faint it's as though he simply forgot to shave this morning, or tug at the front of his shirt, clammy with sweat. He nags at Middlesex, who seldom answer back. Within an hour, Robinson has also got rid of Gubbins, caught fabulously and one-handed at gully; Malan, another victim for Brown; Paul

Stirling, who shuffles across and is lbw; and Stevie Eskinazi, bamboozled before offering another outside edge.

I think about R. C. Robertson-Glasgow, who relished coming to Hove with Somerset. He liked that 'something' in the sea air, a blessing for the 'swerving bowler'. He liked the nearby pub, where the pros could 'meditate' over a pint, contemplating a day's play during 'vast silences'. Most of all, he liked the fact that tail-enders in teams with quality batting line-ups could go off to the beach and rent themselves a deckchair for a few hours, supremely confident that their services would not be required until the total passed 450 or 500 and the captain declared.

If Middlesex's tail-enders had done this today, someone would now be panicking, sending out a search party and telephoning for a taxi to ferry them back here. For Robinson is on a royal roll. It is one of those spells he will remember until his last breath. James Harris lasts just two balls before perishing in the slips. John Simpson is clean bowled, the ball flicking the top of off stump. Nathan Sowter gifts Brown a hat-trick of catches.

I move from the South Stand to the dozen or so slatted wooden seats that lie in a wedge of grass next to the dressing rooms. The grass has been allowed to grow a little long here. It is speckled with daises and dandelions. Cabbage white butterflies weave overhead, looking for somewhere to perch. Were it not for the sight of the 450ft British Airways i360 tower, which is planted on the seafront and looks like a posh factory chimney, being here would feel rather like watching a match in a park. Middlesex's batsmen come and go, the silence of optimistic entrance and sorrowful exit broken only by polite applause and the scrape of their spikes against the stone steps.

On the bookseller's stall I had found a copy of *A Sussex Cricket Odyssey*, a softback lovingly self-published. The author, Laetitia Stapleton, was a member at Hove for more than half a century. She saw her first game there in 1921 when Sussex, like almost everyone else, lost to Warwick Armstrong's Australians. In those days, bygone to us, she remembered how 'severely segregated' women were inside the ground. They were given 'hard and uncomfortable chairs' in a spot called 'the hen coop'. It was the 'era of cloth caps and braces' for the men, who were often 'worse for the amount they had imbibed'. There were hats, 'long dresses and gloves' for the women. What I like most is her description of something that seems charmingly eccentric in our era of perpetual communication: Stapleton writes of the 'telegraph boy' who would wait at the players' gate until the end of an over and then go on a 'sprightly sprint' to hand over an orange envelope. 'Sometimes the player would stuff the wire straight into his pocket . . . sometimes the recipient . . . would survey the contents with some thought,' she said. The crowd, Stapleton added, would speculate about the contents. 'Had there been a disaster at home? Had a child been born? Had someone been chosen to play for England? Or was it just the result of the 2.30 [race]?' Lionel, Lord Tennyson, the captain of Hampshire, frequently sent telegrams to his players while he watched them bat. One of them, who had just missed a short ball and had been hit around the heart, got the unsupportive message: 'What do you think your _____ bat is for?' Another, struggling against an attack Tennyson considered puny, was ordered: 'For God's sake get out and let someone else take a hundred off this jam.'

Middlesex's captain is Malan. Any telegram from him would surely comprise only one word. It would be 'Help'. His team are 44 for eight. It is difficult for me to believe not only that Middlesex are in this state in Division Two, promotion again unlikely for them, but also that I saw them win the County Championship at Lord's less than three years ago, a September day so hot and dusty that it felt like mid-July.

Only a month ago, Ollie Robinson received his first international call-up at 25 years old. He played for England Lions against an Australian XI at Canterbury, a side that included the Ashes captain Tim Paine. Robinson's match figures were unimpressive – one for 139 – but his selection was unarguable on the basis of his contribution to Sussex, the county who rescued him. In 2014, Robinson was released by Yorkshire for what *The Cricketers' Who's Who* delicately describes as 'a number of unprofessional actions'. He flitted around the Hampshire and Essex Second XIs before Sussex gave him a short-term contract. The rest has been gravy for him. On debut he made a century. Less than a month later he took what was then his career best, six for 33.

In this spell, Robinson has already surpassed that landmark and also reached 200 Championship wickets. He has 48 for the season – 18 of them against Middlesex – at an average of fractionally above 15. We are all beginning to dwell on the record books. Just one Sussex bowler, Cyril Bland, has taken all ten in a first-class innings, accomplishing it coincidentally in the same season as Ranji's 3,000 runs (perhaps the Palace Pier, appearing out of the waves, inspired both of them during that memorable summer). Only 79* bowlers have ever pulled off the feat, able afterwards to wear those wickets like a medal. Robinson would find himself among the elite beside Hedley Verity and Colin Blythe, Clarrie Grimmett and Tich Freeman and Jim Laker and Eric Hollies.

At 4 p.m. the crowd is certain – as Robinson is himself – that he's snatched a ninth wicket, lifting him on to the last step of cricketing history. The long and throaty appeal against Toby Roland-Jones seems the prelude to another celebration. The ball thwacks against the pad. Roland-Jones is bang in front. We wait for confirmation of what we know is fact. We let out a low groan when we don't get it. What looks stone-dead is turned down, a small shake of the head ruining everything. Robinson is incredulous, disgruntled and soon in a chuntering huff at the injustice. If the ball was missing – and I don't believe that – the margin must have been infinitesimal,

---

* Taking all ten wickets in an innings has happened on 82 occasions, but three bowlers – Hedley Verity, Tich Freeman and Jim Laker – have done it twice.

thinner than a hair on a dog's hind leg. In those few seconds Robinson is denied what we'd come to assume is his destiny.

Tom Haines is a bits-and-pieces medium pacer. He is bowling only because the Sussex attack is low on manpower. He has taken only five wickets in 13 previous games. His sixth – he gets Roland-Jones – pushes us back on to our seats in disappointment. We seethe for Robinson, who might never come so close again.

The tenth wicket falls to the leg-spinner Will Beer. Middlesex are 75 all out in 21.4 overs, an outcome that isn't so much defeat against the bowling as debasement. Robinson has taken eight for 24, the best Championship figures of the season so far.

We stand to applaud the conqueror long before he crosses the square.

When Groucho Marx was taken to a County Championship match at Lord's, he sat watching it for an hour or two before asking: 'When does it start?' He could not conceive a contest could go on for days without anyone winning it. He could not conceive either how satisfaction, let alone glory, could possibly come out of it. But it can and it does; Hove and Scarborough demonstrated that even to the most sceptical.

The Yorkshire–Surrey game produced a classic finale, the closing minutes making all that had gone before relevant and worthwhile. At 3.30 p.m. on the last day, shortly before tea, Surrey were 157 for two in pursuit of 318, the target achievable if the slightly slow pitch didn't betray them and some lusty hits paid off. Some of the crowd, seeing only a stalemate ahead, decided to go home, bidding farewell to friends with gratitude for their company. And then, as it so often does, the unexpected occurred out of nothing, the game catching alight. A slack shot. A silly run-out. A stump ripped out and sent on a dance towards the wicketkeeper. Surrey, suddenly five down, had to think about survival rather than success. When the ninth wicket fell, it brought together the grizzled old hand and the new boy. At one end was the 41 year-old Gareth Batty, Bradford born, who made his Championship debut in the year that Princess Diana died. At the other was Jamie Smith, only 18. The pair were still together 53 balls later, preparing for the penultimate over. Those of us who were there will tell you about the hush, the sort of whispering silence that libraries used to enforce.

In came Duanne Olivier. Batty edged his first delivery, surviving miraculously when the ball flew off without giving anyone the chance to claim it. After such a close shave, you could only question afterwards – as Batty surely did – why the second delivery tempted him. He could have left it alone. Did he misjudge the line or lose his bearings? The catch squirted at speed into the slips where Adam Lyth waited with cupped hands. Yorkshire, winners by 123 runs, celebrated as though the Championship was theirs, hugging and wildly high-fiving one another. A game that began at 11 a.m. on a Sunday had ended at 5.56 p.m. on a Wednesday with ten balls to spare. Everything that is good, and everything that is worth preserving about the Championship, was contained in that fluctuating match of 40 wickets and 1,235 runs. It was a poster advertisement for the game.

I think the same about Robinson's performance, a bobby-dazzler.

He is stopped before reaching the gate in front of the dressing rooms and awarded his county cap. The simple presentation is a delight, since Robinson isn't expecting it, but the process always seems to me to be an anomaly in modern cricket. It harks back to those seasons when the professionals travelled second class and stayed in third-rate hotels and the amateurs had 'Mr' prefixing their names on the scorecard. There is something uncomfortably feudal to me about this business. The number of appearances, or the number of runs scored and wickets taken, ought to determine who gets their cap and when; not discretion and subjectivity. Look at Robinson's figures. He deserved these blue quarters of cloth before now.

He takes the cap from his captain and briefly examines it before putting it on to his head and pulling down the peak. It fits him. He trades handshakes and slaps on the back and begins posing for photographs.

I look around, breathing the scene in and listening to the ovation for him. The afternoon glows. We are beneath a sky without cloud. We are in a ground that is a lovely little piece of England. The sea is not far off.

Who would want to be anywhere else but here? How could a summer Sunday possibly be better spent?

Headingley '19: Ben Stokes has a moment to himself,
champagne at the ready

CHAPTER FIVE

We'll Get 'Em in Sixes and Fours

*A last-minute ticket for the match. The view from the top
tier. Abject, pathetic, gutless. The best shot of the
season. Remembering an old Ashes soldier. All the yesterdays
and all the tomorrows of Test cricket.*

Sometimes the end is the only place to start from. To understand the Third Ashes Test at Headingley, which may or may
not be the greatest ever staged anywhere, you have to immediately fast-forward to the last roaring scenes of it – an hour
of cricket when so much happened that you needed a week
afterwards to take everything in. If your allegiance was to
Australia, you needed at least two weeks.

The result was completely preposterous, but not a fluke.
We couldn't analyse it soberly at first because too much emo-

tion got in the way, making the search for rational explanations impossible. We were perfectly aware of what we had seen, but much of it still made no sense. Some of us feel that way even now, despite watching the highlights and pressing the rewind button until it broke.

'Now, what I want is facts.' Charles Dickens was fond of saying this, arguing that the mere possession of the nuts and bolts allowed him to interpret the structure they held together. But the facts of this Test, found in cold type on the scorecard, aren't sufficient on their own to tell the human soap opera of a match, which wove around Ben Stokes. Facts certainly can't convey properly what Stokes did – only the circumstances and the context that led him to do it. Even his own wagon wheel, from which you can extrapolate so much, doesn't express the heft and the weight, the ingenuity and the eloquent destruction of his shots, the very best of which trailed exclamation marks behind them.

While the whole question of where genius comes from is a mystery, you can always recognise the thing when it appears. The spectacle Stokes produced was a revelation of talent. Genius is supposed to have a limit too. Not for Stokes. Not, at any rate, on August 25, 2019. He pushed what he possesses to a new level, astonishing us. Eventually he made you believe that the impossible was always the most likely thing to happen.

In doing so, Stokes hushed Headingley at one moment into the sort of silence in which you could hear only the tick of your own heart or the thump of his bat in the blockhole. In the next, the screaming was like white noise, language secondary to sign and gesture because no one could speak in coherent sentences. There was also the tension of waiting for each ball to be bowled. There was the anxiety of what could occur after it had been. There was a full sun in a serene sky. There were the hard wedges of shadow it cast. There was Time, slipping by and gone before you knew it because every minute was choked with incident: a four, a six, a catch grassed or dropping just short, a run-out hopelessly fumbled, a failed review or pleading appeal. We learned that nothing is more tangible than the present.

You will know, perhaps very well, the details of how odds and common logic were defied. It is necessary to fill space by repeating the day-by-day unfolding of them only because the dance we saw on that final Sunday afternoon was choreographed by everything that went before.

How Australia, lacking Steve Smith, were bowled out for an inadequate 179.

How England, one-nil down in the series, capitulated in reply for just 67 in only 27.5 overs. That total was so paltry, the performance so supine, that suggestions the old country ought to pack in Tests forthwith didn't seem outrageously out of proportion with the level of the crisis. 'NO FIGHT, NO IDEA, NO HOPE', was the headline in *The Times*. The *Daily Mail* was more damning still: 'ABJECT, PATHETIC, GUTLESS'. Each verdict was unarguable on the basis of the evidence.

How Australia roused themselves a little to make 246, setting England a target of 359 to win.

How that total, surpassed only on ten previous occasions in Test history, looked so far off as to be unreachable after the earlier failure of will and basic technique.

How, during that beltingly hot fourth morning, which England began on 156 for three – 203 runs short – the only sensible bet was on Australia, a shiny new ball awaiting them in eight overs.

And how England sank from 238 for four at lunch to 286 for nine in mid-afternoon, still 71 adrift.

On the way into Headingley, I passed a ticket tout at the top of St Michael's Road. He was a corpulent man of late middle age, his bulk sweating already in the heat. His black T-shirt swelled over his belly and a thick lank of hair stuck to his balding head. He gave the punters a typical seller's pitch. 'Don't miss the unforgettable day to come,' he shouted, ostentatiously waving about what he had to offer. 'See England's glory. Watch us make the Aussies weep.'

As nonsensical as this sounds, I had the most peculiar hunch, as inexplicable to me now as it was then, that he'd be proved right.

I had heard the Test described as a complete sell-out so often that I hadn't bothered to enquire about tickets. It was only during the last half-hour of the third day, which I caught on

Sky Sports, that Michael Atherton announced on commentary that 'some seats' were still available in what Yorkshire had demolished, rebuilt and then rechristened the Emerald Stand. For the locals, who know what was there before, it will for ever remain The Football Stand. Its reinvention is nonetheless majestic. Something ramshackle and decrepit, resembling a long wooden 'shed', has become concrete and magnificently polished glass. The design – based on the simplicity of bold, clean lines – transformed the look and feel of Headingley as soon as the last slab was laid and the last pane put in. I had watched the construction go slowly up the previous summer, the banging and drilling an irritating accompaniment to County Championship matches. I was impressed by the way it soared, but didn't appreciate until I got up to the top tier how far below everything would be. I found myself on the front row. I felt like James Stewart's protagonist in Hitchcock's *Vertigo*, afraid to look down in case the earth began to tilt and spin. I liked to sit in the old Football Stand, which offered a prime view. It also meant I was looking out *from* it, rather than *at* it, avoiding the eyesore of ancient wood and corrugated iron. Whereas before only the steeple of St Michael and All Angels church had been visible above the East Pavilion, I now saw the tower as well. I also saw the tip of another church, St Chad's, which I hadn't known existed. Sloping gently upwards behind the Western Terrace was a forest of chimneys, once feathered with smoke, on red-brick terraced houses that were built when Herbert Sutcliffe was nowt but a lad. That morning, between overs, I witnessed the great stir of people in that part of the ground. They were either bringing back pale lager in plastic pots or going to fetch it.

I had never known a Headingley atmosphere like it. Normally brashly raucous, like the beery hubbub of a pub shortly before last orders, the place had a discernible, Lord's-like hum about it. This hum, which was very loud, conveyed anticipation, but also an edgy nervousness that was all about the highest of hopes going unfulfilled. As Joe Root got out, and Jonny Bairstow came in to join Ben Stokes, it intensified rather than abated.

We studied Stokes, wondering what was really going through his mind. He subjugated his normal, swashbuckling approach in deference to defence. He was in it for the long haul. Even when a bouncer crashed into his helmet, and even when a ball beat him and the Australians sucked in their breath and threw up their hands in mock horror at his escape, Stokes went unperturbedly on, protecting his stumps as if he owned nothing more precious in life.

When you're safely in some lavish shade, you tend to forget the temperature as noon approaches. The sweat poured off those exposed to the bullying sun. Occasionally Stokes had to whip off his helmet and wipe his face and forehead with a sweep of one of those muscular, tattooed arms and you admired his application and his concentration in such overbearing conditions. In the World Cup final against New Zealand, fought out only 42 days before, we'd seen how

Stokes could dig in and be different, prepared to wait for the wayward delivery and take runs judiciously in ones and twos until it arrived. He isn't just a showman or show-off; he'll fight until the last dog dies. In that opening session, Stokes consolidated what England had made, content to let Bairstow take the lead until something irresistibly juicy came along for him.

I thought about the first Ashes Test I ever saw. It was at Nottingham in 1972, the only drawn match of a drawn series. That experience could not have been more different; I watched the game, my knees grass-stained, on the boundary. The playing area at Trent Bridge was much bigger then than it is now. For three days I lay beside the rope, waiting for the ball to come close enough so that I could chase it down and retrieve it with an impressive swoop. Just once, after a drive through extra cover from Keith Stackpole, it hopped conveniently into my hands. I had always planned to throw it back, low and flat, directly over the stumps, almost trimming the bails. It didn't quite happen like that; my arm wasn't strong enough to chuck it far. I lobbed the ball underarm, not wanting to make a cack-handed shambles of it. The fielder sent to retrieve the shot, Peter Lever, acknowledged his thanks by lifting his hand politely towards me. The thrill of holding the ball for a few seconds, and seeing the gold leaf of the maker's name gleaming across the smooth leather, was another reward. The price of admission was £1.50 per day, busting the bank of my week's pocket money. I was obliged to ask for a parental loan, collecting a stub of paper at the turnstiles no more substantial than a bus ticket. The ticket for the Emerald Stand – my name and address stamped on the back of it – cost £130, an amount even inflation can't fully explain. Only with hindsight did it strike me as peanuts.

Before the Test began, the *Sydney Morning Herald's* Malcolm Knox wrote a perceptive article about Australia's successes and failures at Headingley. He cited the old ground's 'unique magic'. Knox was spot on in calling Headingley 'eccentric in shape and unpredictable in its outcomes'. He celebrated the Yorkshire team of 1902 that scuttled the tourists – 'Victor Trumper and all' – for 23. He went back to 1975, the pitch dug up by vandals making a selfish public protest, unconnected to cricket, and denying Rick McCosker the measly five runs he needed for a century. Knox mentioned only in passing – as if it still caused Australia anguish to dwell on it – the Test of 1981. Ian Botham whacking the ball 'into the confectionery stall and out again'. Bob Willis's demonic bowling. The bookmaker, rashly offering 500–1 on England as a publicity stunt, and then sobbing into his cash till afterwards. The main purpose of the feature focused on the fourth Test of the 1948 series, the match in which Arthur Morris fought his way to 182 in 291 minutes and shared in a stand of 301 with Donald Bradman. Australia scored 404 on a wearing pitch in less than a day. No team had made a higher fourth-innings total to win a Test, the record standing for 28 years. 'It was at wild, woolly Headingley that the invincibility of the 1948 Australians became a fact,' said Knox, a pay-off line honouring Morris that only a pedant would dispute. There wasn't a blemish in the piece, which I lapped up like milk, but the graphic illustrating it, supposedly pointing out where Headingley sits on the map of England, placed Leeds north of York and somewhere between Ripon and Thirsk. As this Ashes Test played itself out, I remembered the mistake, thinking it unintentionally symbolised how disorientated Australia can get when the pressure is on here.

History never repeats itself, but man always does. The modern cricketer can access every bit of information about himself and the opposition, the clips of film and the myriad charts available with a click of his laptop or iPad. The Australian captain Tim Paine ought to have tapped into the archives and swotted up on the 1981 Test. He could have avoided the trap that Kim Hughes tumbled into 38 years before.

A shower of wickets fell in the afternoon: Bairstow darted at a wide ball; Buttler was needlessly run out because of Ben Stokes's yes–no dithering; Woakes pushed a doddle of a catch into the covers; Archer holed out in the deep; and Broad was struck on the boot in front of his stumps. Australia's retention of the Ashes was a formality.

I had abandoned the front row of the Emerald Stand during lunch; I'd become too squeamish about the low rail in front of me and the long drop below it. I stood on the concourse of the bottom tier, beside whooping Australians, before finding an abandoned seat. An Australian next to me, already obnoxiously drunk, took a swig at his beer and drained it to the dregs, wiping his wet lips with the sleeve of his T-shirt. He rushed immediately back to the bar. 'I want something to toast the boys when we take you down,' he said, tipping his cap. He staggered away, listing slightly. I never saw him again.

The incoming batsman at Headingley has to walk along a dark corridor and up a small flight of steps to get on to the field and into the sunshine. Out came Jack Leach, attired for the scrap as last man with arm guard, thigh protector and bulky padding beneath his shirt. We didn't know it then, but the cavalry had arrived; Stokes didn't have to shoot his way out of difficulty alone.

As soon as Leach took 92 off Ireland at Lord's in July, so becoming a better class of nightwatchman, he found himself likened to David Steele, a fellow wearer of glasses. More than a generation and a half ago, Steele gained cult-celebrity status and the sobriquet 'The Bank Clerk Who Went to War' for repeatedly showing the full blade of his Duncan Fearnley to Lillee and Thomson. Like Steele, Leach can stick obdurately around for hours at the crease, eventually glazing your eyes like crockery. Like Steele, he is an incongruous sight in pads. And, also like Steele, he is more Reformation man than Renaissance dandy. I look at Leach nevertheless and I think of Bill Bowes. The pair, born three generations apart, are similar in innocuous appearance and also in attitude, approach, application and, above all, persistence. Leach grafts hard for everything in the same way that Bowes did.

Of the 62 balls it took England to inexplicably crack Australia apart, Leach faced only 17 and squeezed out just one run, a nudge off his hip that brought the scores level. He ignored what he didn't have to play. He ducked what could have hit him. He tackled with a dead-bat what had to be kept out. Strange as it seems, the Australians were left with more puzzled wrinkles over Leach than over Stokes. This was only because everyone knew what Stokes could do if the mood seized him. As soon as he decided to go on the attack, treating that last session like a Twenty20 run chase, everything was accomplished with a tremendous clarity of thought and deed. He intimidated Australia before he dominated them.

But Leach?

He revealed qualities we didn't know he possessed; and perhaps he didn't know he possessed them to such an extent either. We will always remember that Stokes couldn't flick a glance at either the ball or his partner from the non-striker's end. He either crouched down, the bat between his legs so that he looked like a medieval knight resting on his sword, or bent himself double to avoid eye contact.

Bowes used to clean his glasses with a handkerchief or the front tails of his shirt, which would be tugged out of his flannels. Leach relies on a dark cloth. As he got it out of his pocket, and began rubbing the lenses, his role at the heart of the drama seemed more surreal than ever, as if he'd wandered in from a club game that had finished early. Paine's Australians, dazed by this, were like Hughes's team against Botham. Nothing can change until it is faced. And in both cases, though decades apart, the mistakes made by Hughes were also made by Paine. You knew that only in retrospect because the dazzle of the central batting performance obscured everything else while it took place.

Australia assumed too much, convincing themselves that the law of averages – the need to be lucky just once – was so loaded in their favour that they simply had to wait for it to take effect.

It is hard to know precisely when they cottoned on, aware at last that statistical probability alone would not deliver the Test to them. Perhaps it was when Stokes lifted Nathan Lyon over mid-off. Perhaps it was when he did it again. Or perhaps, more likely, it was that exquisite reverse sweep, the execution of which began a half-breath before Lyon released the ball. You saw Stokes pivot into position and turn his strong wrists. His left leg was planted down the pitch. His head was still. Every movement was so rapid, and the ball was struck so ferociously, that Stokes momentarily unbalanced himself. He lost his footing and slid a little, like someone on a shiny patch of ice. But the ball had already gone by then, dismissed from his presence; you followed the flight of it, a high black dot against the shiny sky. The shot was taken by an anonymous pair of hands in the eighth row of the Western Terrace.

In the last session of the previous day, Stokes had made two runs off 50 balls. He had taken a further 69 deliveries to add 30 to his score. When Leach came in, he was on 61 off 174. Now, plugged in and lit up, Stokes did whatever he liked – cutting, pulling, driving, improvising. Paine cast the field wide and deep for him, scattering men in likely places. He did so like a gambler spread-betting in the hope of limiting his losses. Stokes either found a gap or bashed the ball casually into the belly of the crowd. There was an audacious scoop shot, off Pat Cummins, that shone like a bar of gold; Stokes skipped outside off stump and swung the ball to fine leg. There was also a savage pull to bring up his century – his 199th ball – after Josh Hazle-wood loosely dropped a delivery in the slot for him.

The corking stroke of Stokes's that will always stay with me is nevertheless the one which came next. It was of the sort that fastens your eyelids open, making it momentarily impossible to blink. After bowling too short, Hazlewood tried to compensate and consequently bowled too full. Speared in at middle and leg, it came to Stokes just above his left ankle. You have to be seeing the ball as though it's the size of a Belisha beacon – and it has to glow like one as well – to do what Stokes did. He instinctively sank on to his left knee and sent the full toss over the square-leg boundary. His timing was impeccable. His shot with that strong bottom-hand grip was so languid as to seem effortless, the contact he made no more than a sweet caress flush off the middle of the bat. Shading his eyes as he followed the shot, Hazlewood was dumbfounded. So was

Marnus Labuschagne, who for a second or two readied himself for a catch. Again, someone in the Western Terrace gleefully claimed the ball on the first bounce, the fielder redundant.

With Ben Stokes and Jack Leach roped together like climbers, each dependent on the other for survival, the big electronic scoreboard counted England home. From 59 to 50. From 40 to 33. From 27 to 19. Still no bright ideas were hatched against Stokes; and Australia didn't slow down the rate sufficiently to properly compose themselves and think of one. The Test was being played at the pace Stokes set, which is why it spun tumultuously out of Tim Paine's control. In the confusion the bowlers abetted their own defeat with a surprising loss of poise and gumption – too short, too wide, a curious lack of yorkers. Without contradicting that assessment of their failings, which were many, we can press the point that, despite everything, Australia still ought to have won. Every memory of Headingley that afternoon will consequently carry a sharp edge for them. None, though, will be sharper than the chances of redemption that were fluffed or cocked up, each mistake ghastlier than the last.

England needed 17. We were at the stage in which some people could not look and others watched through the gaps between their fingers. No one moved. Not much was said; we bit our bottom lips rather than let our tongues blurt out a prediction. Drinkers let their beer go flat, warm and untouched. Mobile phones went unused, the rarity of that sight one for collectors of trivia.

Though truly self-assured, with few doubts, Stokes had come unscathed through the odd scrape and the occasional misjudgment. He had a swish and missed, wafting his bat through the hot air. He went after one delivery and bottom-edged it on to his pads rather than on to the bails. And, after flashing hard at a wide ball from Cummins, we watched a thick top edge loop towards Marcus Harris, dashing in from third man. Harris was running into the low sun, his mirrored glasses reflecting the whole ground ahead of him. His shadow was as thin as a spike. During the nine strides Harris took, we saw the entire match flash in front of us. Our eyes bulged, our mouths gaped open and we clasped our hands to our cheeks in 20,000-odd reproductions of *The Scream*, each of us imitating the horror in Munch's canvas. Harris dived full-length for the ball, his right hand outstretched as though in a plea for it. The catch went into his palm and slipped out again, his elbow jarring it free from his fingers as his arm bumped into the grass. His body slithered forward, bringing up a huge divot of turf. Harris lay still for a short while after stopping, reluctant to pick himself up again and go back on to the rope.

We thought England would be safe from then on. How wrong we were.

With eight to win, Paine, who seemed to see these things

with his eyes wide shut, squandered Australia's last review after a delivery from Cummins to Leach pitched a foot outside leg stump, rapping the pad. The lbw review, born of the fear of imminent defeat, contained no grain of serious optimism, striking you at the time as a foolhardy waste. Of course, not long afterwards, it became much more than that.

Coincidence and implausibility are said to be God's way of remaining anonymous. Anyone with a better explanation of what came next should offer it to Paine.

Earlier in the match Stokes came on to bowl, sending down 24 consecutive overs, when Jofra Archer was cramping and Stuart Broad and Chris Woakes had run out of puff. He held up the attack the way Superman holds up a bridge that is about to collapse. Exceptional talent is only one of the reasons he can do that. The other is his work ethic. Stokes slogs and sweats when we aren't looking so he can perform his miracles in front of us later. Remember the catch he took in the opening World Cup game against South Africa at The Oval? Remember his double-century, also against them, for England in Cape Town? Practice makes Stokes what he is. What physical effort can't polish is his running between the wickets. He can be Boycott-esque in this regard.

With two runs needed, Stokes reverse-swept Lyon. The shuffle he straight away took down the track acted like a starting pistol on Leach. He was halfway down, stranded in cricket's no-man's-land, when Stokes abruptly turned his back on him and retreated. Leach could see from there what Stokes had already registered from the crease. The shot had found Cummins. Leach swivelled on his heels, knowing as he did so that his feet were never going to move faster along the ground than the ball would move through the air. He was hurling himself at the line, like a sprinter for the tape, when Cummins's throw whooshed towards his end. By then Leach was still so shy of where he ought to be that he could comfortably have been run out twice. The throw fell short of Lyon, skipping off the pitch and coming at him at waist height. He grabbed for it. A mere two steps separated him from the stumps. In getting there, Lyon left the ball behind – a consequence of nerves and of panic. Someone's tragedy is always someone else's comedy; the Western Terrace ridiculed him ruthlessly.

Lyon will re-experience that moment from now until the day he meets his maker. It will be a haunting he'll never quite exorcise. He'll have anxiety dreams about it, like the sort in which you are falling from a tall building or your teeth drop out. In those dreams Lyon will understand, without entirely realising why, that whatever he does will make no difference to the outcome. His subconscious will eventually remind him that he's been here before – and that he's failed before too, a fate he is now doomed to repeat. The ball will disintegrate as soon as it touches his hand, leaving red dust on his fingers. Or he'll look up and find the stumps, beside him a split second ago, are now 200 feet away. Or the ground will break up and he'll take a slapstick pratfall into the hole. But – and this is far worse – there will be other dreams that become nightmares for him only once they are over. These are the dreams in which his shadow-self will actually succeed. His take will be clean. He will reach the stumps with Leach nowhere to be seen. Lyon will find himself in a celebratory hug with his teammates. For a minute or so, the ecstasy of that will be overwhelming. Then he will awaken with a snap at three o'clock in the morning, the cold of the night around him. For the next hour, the whole damn wretched thing will thump about in his head again, making sleep impossible.

I swear one Australian, wearing a supporters' cap and shirt, began to sob. Another put his hands on his head and looked into the high blue curve of the sky. A third, in a turmoil of feeling, put her hands on her knees, stared at the floor and wailed: 'No'. Lyon went back to his mark to complete the over. Until he bowled it, we assumed nothing else could shock us in this convulsing Test.

Coming around the wicket to seek rehabilitation, Lyon was sure he had instantly found it. Stokes went to sweep him conventionally. The ball hit the bottom of the pad. Paine and the fielders around him went off like a box of fireworks. Lyon screamed. The umpire, Joel Wilson, looked at him from beneath the brim of his straw hat. He held a dignified pose, hands in front of his body, and shook his head. Lyon dropped on to the pitch, indulging in a bizarre half-roll backwards after the decision went against him.

The replay showed Lyon's delivery taking leg stump. The most sympathetic thing you can say about Wilson's umpiring, here and also in the first Test at Edgbaston, is that he had some off days, proof of human fallibility. It is very possible, however, that Wilson got this decision right and the machine got it wrong. Hawk-Eye sometimes does seem cockeyed to those of us who sit at home on the sofa, grumbling with incredulity when the line and trajectory look – to our eyes, at least – as though technology has given the ball the properties of a magic jumping bean. We may lack a degree in either mathematics or physics, but we have seen a lot of cricket in a lot of places. Stokes felt certain the ball wasn't hitting the stumps. In thinking identically, Wilson surely calculated the percentages in getting lbw when a right-arm spinner is bowling around the wicket at a left-hander, shaping to swipe him leg-side. But, as Paine had already spent his final review so prodigally, the realisation of what he could have won with it left Australia reeling like a bash to the head with some lead piping. Australia gathered themselves up for a last effort, knowing it would be hopeless.

Four balls later, the Test was finally England's.

Jack Leach let the first ball fly over his head. He blocked the second. He pushed away the third, angled in at him from around the wicket, and claimed his single behind square. As long as he plays the game, I don't think Pat Cummins will bowl a worse ball at such a pivotal juncture than the one he sent down to Ben Stokes. It was short. It was wide. Stokes rolled his eyes and looked at it with slavering joy. He heaved his bat and his body through it. Chasing the ball was useless, so Australia didn't bother.

'ENGLAND WIN BY ONE WICKET', said the score-board, as if, amid the pandemonium, we didn't know.

Like all major sports, cricket has cameras everywhere. What we see inside a ground when we are there is shown from half a dozen different angles when we watch it again on TV. The recorded images blend in so seamlessly with the live ones that you almost can't distinguish between the memory of what you saw there and what you witnessed on the box. When I replay that final ball in my mind, I think first of the wide-screen shot, filmed side-on, that I didn't see until much later. It was taken at pitch level. Ben Stokes is framed in the middle distance and on the extreme right; he looks minute against the background of the packed stand. You see him blast Cum-mins's delivery from the crease. You see him throw his arms aloft before the ball is even halfway to the boundary. A nano-second elapses – no more – before the whole of the Western Terrace rises as one behind him like a breaking wave.

When, during their first innings, England went down as passively as captives facing a firing squad, we questioned in disillusion whether Tests would soon be extinct, unable to resist the charge of the white-ball game. Few batsmen seemed to possess the nous to play in them. Doubts about the future of Tests were shed at Headingley. We were considering only where this one rated in the 2,258 staged since 1877. There is no gainsaying historical significance, and we're always being glibly told that this Test or the other will 'never be forgotten'. The value of some inflates, while others' dissipates, as generations bow out. My own has been lucky; we have seen more of them than our predecessors. The first volume of *The Wisden Book of Test Cricket*, which stops in April, 1978, records only 824 Tests. The most recent volume, covering only the years 2009 to 2014, logs 307. Among the Tests that endure are two ties and another two draws with the scores level in the fourth innings. *Wisden* reminds us of how England beat Australia by the narrow squeak of two runs at Edgbaston in 2005. And how, just a dozen years before that, West Indies – also against Australia – triumphed by a single run. Two Ashes Tests have been settled by three runs. A further 18 were decided by either two wickets or fewer than 20 runs.

This will sound biased, since I was there, but I can't think of a more compelling Test, a slow-burn before the explosive conflagration of that finale, which exhausted you with one improbability after another. Stokes got to where he was going – 139 off 219 balls – in such a series of magnificent steps that in retrospect you almost believed it was all part of some wonderful plan he had. Alone on the periphery of the pitch afterwards, he got down on his haunches. It looked as though he was trying to take in what he'd done by shutting out the din around him with silent prayer.

I had the most peculiar thought then. It was about Arthur Morris.

*

He was one of the elder statesmen of Australian cricket for so long that you almost forgot that he'd once been a relatively young, dark-haired man without a crease on his narrow face. I met him only once; he was 87 years old then.

Arthur Morris was sitting alone in the lounge of the Dorset Square Hotel. He wore a baggy oatmeal cardigan and a pair of square steel-framed spectacles. I stared at him from a wary distance, unable to believe the truth my eyes were telling me. I remember that he was reading a copy of the *Daily Telegraph*, which he gripped with thick, strong fingers. After doing some basic research later, I discovered a detail that made our unexpected meeting seem even more serendipitous. The date – July 25, 2009 – coincided with the anniversary of that First Miracle of Headingley in 1948.

I mumbled something pathetically inadequate as an excuse for bothering him. Morris lowered his newspaper and looked at me with kindly solicitude, immediately confirming what I had heard about him: he was a first-class gentleman with impeccably first-rate manners. I would love to report that I gently interrogated him with questions of blazing perspicuity. Alas, not. I was a little star-struck. I said nothing, I'm certain, that Morris hadn't heard innumerable times in innumerable places. I explained to him that Headingley was my 'home ground'. 'Not the prettiest,' he said, 'but I liked it because Yorkshire knows its cricket and Yorkshiremen appreciated what you did – providing you did it well. The atmosphere was different from anywhere else.

The cricket truly meant something to the folk who were there.'

Donald Bradman thought Morris 'wasn't always straight in defence' but believed that fact was 'merely a sign of his genius' (that assessment could apply to Steve Smith, who takes the MCC's coaching manual and makes abstract art out of it).

Morris still accomplished much. He rose to become Australia's vice-captain and, briefly, captain. With New South Wales, he won five post-war Sheffield Shield titles. He made 3,533 runs at 46.48 in 46 Tests. Even his quirks were charming. Morris liked to listen to records when his team-mates batted, bringing his own phonograph into the dressing room. When Lindsay Hassett was dismissed for some piddlingly low score, Morris marked his return to the pavilion by putting on 'My Defences Are Down' from the musical *Annie Get Your Gun*. He was also never the kind of cricketer – and there are a goodly number of them – who rated the dead so highly that the living never stood a chance. Only a few pernickety points of modern terminology seemed to bother him. 'I always think of batsmen. Now they tell me they're batters,' he said. 'Batter is something you put on fish.'

Morris died in 2015, aged 93. His obituaries were generous and respectful, full of his innings at Headingley in 1948. I realised, as I read them, that I had miserably failed to ask him the obvious question: how did it feel – especially in old age – to be constantly taken back to only one day of such an eventful life? Did it bore him? Did he think of it as a chore?

Did he want to run and hide whenever a stranger loomed over him in a hotel lounge and began discussing Headingley again?

I will never find out, but I am aware of this. Ben Stokes will always be asked to relive his innings – whether he likes it or not. On every significant anniversary of the Test – put a date in your 2044 and 2069 diaries – he will write books and make documentaries about it. He will be applauded at dinners and during reunions. In both 25 and 50 years from now, he will be interviewed at length for whatever passes as print journalism by then. In the meantime, during quiet mornings when he probably wants to be on his own, he will have to patiently tolerate some bothersome 'fan', just like me, who barges up to him and says: 'Headingley 2019. Can you tell me about it?'

Being a hero can be difficult.

Myths grow around great events when the truth about them is too mundane. We need to make a grander and taller peg on which the story can hang. So we look for some embellishment that befits the achievement. We demand the kind of legend in which we can honestly believe and pass on into the ages.

When the last man, Wilfred Rhodes, walked out to meet George Hirst at The Oval in 1902, England required 15 runs to beat Australia. Hirst is supposed to have uttered one of the best-known lines in cricket. 'We'll get 'em in singles.' It was hogwash, a bit of whimsy from some anonymous press-box scribe with a novelist's imagination. The words stuck, nevertheless. Everyone wanted those words to be fact even before constant repetition – and wishing – made them so. This persisted even after Rhodes attempted, as late as his nineties, to nail the fib.

Headingley 2019 has the stories of how, afterwards, Ben Stokes went to a burger restaurant and ate fish and how Jack Leach guaranteed himself free optical treatment and spectacles for life. What it lacks is dialogue to rival Hirst's and Rhodes's. Leach struggled to remember vaguely, let alone verbatim, what Stokes said to him after he came in. Stokes insisted coyly that he'd only 'sort of' laid out a tactical plan to his partner, the scale and compass points of it nebulous.

We can do better than that . . .

Of the 76-run partnership, Stokes hit 74. There were seven sixes and four fours. So surely Stokes must have said to Leach, 'We'll get 'em in sixes and fours'. Not only because that is precisely what he did, but also because the declaration exactly matches our image of the man himself, his character and the ideal he presents to us. And if he didn't say it . . . well, he ought to have done, which makes pretending he did legitimate.

There, it's done; I look forward to seeing Stokes's words in the next edition of the *Oxford Dictionary of Quotations*.

The gift of speed in an unlikely setting.
Jofra Archer bowling in the Sussex countryside.

CHAPTER SIX

The Scorebook and the Pencil

*Counting the crowd one at a time. The Player Who
Stopped Play. The cloak that hides the dagger. Jofra Archer
and the gift of speed. The County Championship's wild
schemes and wilder notions. A cup of tea in a quiet place.*

At The Oval, Pat Cummins fires in the first delivery of the
fifth Ashes Test, tempting Rory Burns into playing and
missing outside off stump. At the ground formerly known
as Grace Road, now carrying the moniker of Leicestershire's
sponsors, Chris Wright forces Doug Bracewell into a false
shot as well, another flirtation outside off stump. I am listening to Cummins on the radio. I am watching Wright
from the Pavilion End. Because those two balls are bowled
as near as dammit simultaneously, as though everything has

been synchronised for my benefit, the 102 miles separating the East Midlands from south London seem to collapse around me. The geography and the matches become distorted, suddenly blending into one another. I'm not exactly sure whether I'm here or there – or somewhere in between. The confusion, lasting for only a second or two, ends when I yank out the earpieces of my radio. Gone is the hubbub of the crowd at the Test. I hear instead some gentle hand clapping, the respectful sort that you get at a village fete after the speeches are over.

Already, there are almost 25,000 inside The Oval, where England are trying to recover from defeat at Old Trafford and level the series. There are fewer than 400 of us at the Fischer County Ground. I walked around the stands less than a quarter of an hour before the start, taking my own head count. It came to 378; a few enthusiasts, I suppose, could be hiding from me.

Leicestershire are taking on Northamptonshire, the third day of a contest between one team scraping about at the bottom of the Division Two barrel and another floating not far from the top.

I like to be an early riser where matches are concerned, among the first to get through the gates. Since it is already mid-September, you feel autumn moving in fast. The morning air has a distinct edge to it. I am aware of the heavy, peaty smell of the earth too. A frisky wind is coming in from the north-west, every gust pilfering leaves from the tall trees, among them limes and silver birch, that sit beyond the boundary. Small stacks, copper-brown and brittle, lie against the white picket fence at a corner of the Bennett End and are regularly blown about.

Whatever name is attached to this pinch of land – I prefer Grace Road – it is one of the game's more humble parishes, developed among the gabled Victorian houses that occupy the narrow streets. The architecture is so undistinguished that, without prior intelligence, you would struggle at first sight to identify the pavilion among the hotchpotch of buildings. A little rudimentary sleuthing would be needed because all the stands are plain-looking and so unprepossessingly low that the floodlights, looming above the ground like emaciated iron giants, seem twice as tall as anywhere else on the County Championship circuit. Still standing too, surely for sentimental reasons, is 'The Meet', which resembles a farmyard barn in need of a splash of whitewash. A long building with a curved roof, it was once an open stand at Aylestone Road, the place Leicestershire called home until 1946. The sight of it almost brings back a waft of pre-war cigarette smoke.

You only have to look around to realise that the club is obliged to mend and make do, keeping up appearances as ably as it can because the housekeeping budget only just about covers the necessities. For three successive years Leicestershire recorded a 'small profit'. The most recent balance sheet was bleaker. It revealed a loss of £157,000 and an overall deficit of nearly £300,000.

Leicestershire, living a long while in the doldrums, have not been in Division One since 2003, the year Twenty20 began and, according to *The Times*, provoked 'mild bemusement' among those who went to gawp at the first fixtures as though the circus had a new freak. Since 2011, the county has been like the avid but inadequate contestant in *Bake Off* who seldom lets go of the wooden spoon. Leicestershire have finished bottom five times, including those miserably back-to-back summers of 2014 and 2015, which passed without a solitary win. They are about to finish bottom again. Their only Championship success so far came on the season's opening week, the optimism it generated soon squashed. If this were not dire enough, the team also finished bottom in both their Twenty20 and 50-over qualifying groups.

Given that kind of abysmal form, it is no surprise to find them at the foot of another table. For the past two years, Championship crowds at Grace Road haven't broken five figures: a mere 9,090 saw them in 2017 and only 9,757 came in 2018 when the weather was so glorious that I felt as though I'd taken a Time Machine back to the endless sunshine of 1976. The second-lowest total in that same period – germane because of today's fixture – belongs to Northamptonshire, who pulled in a combined 20,377. Next to those statistics is another that emphasises the upstairs–downstairs world the Championship has become since the ECB chopped it down the middle. Surrey and Yorkshire had gates of over 94,000 apiece, a fact of which Leicestershire and their ilk will be jealously aware. Without the ECB's annual subsidy, a largesse of more than £2 million, Leicestershire would have a hole in the seat of their pants that only the most generous sponsorship could patch.

If this wasn't such a convivial club, the setting and also the circumstances Leicestershire find themselves in would guarantee a melancholy atmosphere. But all the stewards say a cheery 'hello' and mean it . . . the second-hand bookstall relies on an honesty box . . . the waitresses in 'The Meet' amiably treat the customers like friends . . . and the office staff take your money for a scorecard, genuinely grateful that you have bought one. I walked past as a member of the local Cricket Society buttonholed Leicestershire's all-rounder, Neil Dexter, before the start. Would he be 'kind enough' to donate a shirt for the Society's next raffle? 'Of course,' he said, unhesitatingly and with the utmost sincerity.

On the basis of vignettes like that one, I can't but fondly like the place and wish it well. But, as I tune in to *Test Match Special* while witnessing Leicestershire mop up Northants's tail and then bat again themselves, I conclude something else too: the cricket their old boy Jonathan Agnew is colourfully describing from The Oval is so starkly different from the cricket here that the relationship between them is tenuous indeed.

★

Northamptonshire, 325 for seven overnight, add 32 to their total and give themselves a first-innings lead of 49. One ball, from Will Davies, bewilders everyone – especially the batsman, Brett Hutton. The delivery hit off stump without taking the bail; it looked as though someone had superglued it into the groove. This is a bad portent for Leicestershire, who got another soon enough. Just before noon the cloud, which had been swelling for almost an hour, gathered more densely and, exactly like that bail, refused to be dislodged. The floodlights were turned on to cut through the murk.

I still balk a little when I see floodlights on cricket grounds such as Grace Road. Though sleek and polished, no designer has made them acceptable to the eye. You can only console yourself with the thought of how useful something so ugly can be, bringing salvation from the blight of bad light. The bulbs come on in silvery clusters, firstly illuminating the corners of the ground. An old memory is illuminated too. Not long after I began practising Kipling's Black Art – I was on the sports desk of an evening newspaper at last – one of my enjoyable tasks was jotting down the tea scores from the Press Association's 'rip-and-read' teleprinter before dropping them down the chute that connected the editorial floor to the composing room. The scores were printed in the Stop Press of the Late Final, the edition bespoke for the home-ward-bound commuter (I suspect no one under 35 now knows what the Stop Press was). It was a straightforward but serious assignment. Accuracy was paramount. One of the

newspaper's long-ago small calamities had brought it ridi-
cule, making a collector's item of the Late Final in which it
appeared. In those days, Nottinghamshire had an off-spinner
called Bob White. Tradition dictated that a copytaker would
ring Trent Bridge to take down the latest score and then
bring it to the sports department for checking. On this particular afternoon, self-evidently a gloomy one, the copytaker
misheard the reporter, in the way that the chorus of Bob
Dylan's 'Blowin' in the Wind' is sometimes misheard as 'the
ants are my friends', the ultimate mondegreen. The copytaker's mistake was compounded by the sub-editor's laziness.
He didn't bother to read the slip of paper that was handed
to him. That is why the Stop Press of that day's Late Final
read:

NOTTS 53 for one. BOB WHITE STOPPED PLAY

The story, which sounds apocryphal, is true; the copytaker
responsible was still there when I arrived on the newspaper.
I was told the error had to be explained to her.

Leicestershire's innings, every minute of it under those
lights, does not detain the impatient. It is significant only for
the oddity of eight lbw decisions, equalling the world record
in a first-class innings. Up goes the index finger of either
Paul Pollard or Billy Taylor – and out went the heart and the
rump of what passes for Leicestershire's finest. Barely a
month before, Colin Ackermann had claimed the world's

best Twenty20 bowling figures, taking seven for 18 against the county that in those bun fights calls itself Birmingham Bears. Six of Ackermann's haul came in two overs. Here, he makes 60. The only other serious contribution comes from Neil Dexter. His 42 runs includes a six, which I duck to avoid; I save myself from the possibility of writing this from the infirmary. Dexter is a bit unlucky; Hawk-Eye might have overruled his lbw decision. He goes away with a trudging step.

I had wanted to watch Hassan Azad. On the opening day of the match, he'd crowned his debut season at Grace Road by becoming just the fifth batsman this summer to reach 1,000 runs. Sadly, I arrived too late. The tap producing his scores had gone dry. Azad, who is 25 and made his Championship debut belatedly in April, could hardly get a shot off the cut portion. The ball, hitting him on the pad and also on the thigh, seldom went anywhere near the middle of the bat. It was mystifying. I began to add up the number of deliveries he had faced without scoring. I got to 23 and lost the thread. Azad was dismissed for six, leaving those of us who hadn't seen him before ignorant of his talent. Leicestershire were 189 all out, which was much less of a surprise.

At lunch during the Test, Jonathan Agnew interviewed Trevor Bayliss. It was a valedictory, state-of-the-nation address to mark the end of his tenure as England coach. Bayliss is one of those men who chooses his words with great care and delivers them only after great contemplation. If you were a reporter, dependant for your crust on the saleability of Bayliss quotes, you would be starving and begging in the bread queue within a week. Even walking around Lord's, parading the World Cup, looked akin to torture for someone who so loathes the limelight. Bayliss spoke now out of obligation; he saw it as a duty to leave his thoughts behind before returning to Australia.

What Bayliss said to Agnew, he would say again – more expansively – to others, but the kernel of his advice was this. Cut the amount of domestic cricket. Prepare flatter pitches so batsmen learn how to bed down on them and spinners become as significant as dibbly-dobbly seamers. Twist the calendar about so the County Championship is no longer predominantly played at opposite poles of the season. Bayliss didn't make plain his belief that a Championship of 18 counties is unfit for purpose, too bloated and uncompetitive to successfully nurture tomorrow's Test stars. He let you draw that conclusion for yourself, his message buried subliminally between the lines and behind a few deliberate pauses and hesitations. Bayliss was a little blunter in *The Daily Telegraph*, asking a question so loaded that answering it became superfluous. It was this: 'From a fan's point of view, are you happy to go and watch a standard of cricket that is so-so or go along and see real quality?' For the numbskulls, who still hadn't entirely grasped his point, Bayliss finally cleared his throat and let rip with ESPNcricinfo. 'You have to ask whether the county game is producing the players we need. Is the competition underneath doing the job it should be?' he said. 'There's a huge gap between county and international cricket.' He reiterated the word 'huge' as though italicising it. The nub of his case came next. 'I think there are too many teams. If you had fewer – maybe ten – the best players would be in competition against each other more often and the standard would rise . . . you'd see tougher cricketers develop.' With a lot of nodding and winking, he was offering us the model of Australia's Sheffield Shield, where six sides play ten matches apiece before the top two slug it out in a final.

No doubt, if he had been sitting next to me, Bayliss would have looked across Grace Road and felt vindicated in his small campaign for reform. Leicestershire versus Northamptonshire demonstrates in microcosm the demographic problem the Championship faces. Here are knots of men – there are few women – well beyond pensionable age, and so freed from the encumbrance of the nine-to-five working week. Each wears a mid-length padded coat with lots of pockets or a thickish sweater and a hat or cap of some kind. Each carries a rucksack or bag, no doubt containing one or more of the following: sandwiches in a plastic box, bottled water, a Thermos flask, a cricket reference book, a pair of binoculars, a newspaper and a miniature radio. Anyone who goes regularly to the Championship would identify them as cricket watchers from twenty furlongs away. I often say that I merely go to games to feel a little young again; I am not necessarily exaggerating.

The urgent need for Leicestershire to turn a penny, however it can, is apparent too. In 'The Meet' I find out-of-date posters, advertising the open-air screening of Hollywood films at Grace Road, and fresh ones that promote a forthcoming fireworks extravaganza and also a murder-mystery evening.

The even harder task of competing on the field is apparent near one of the main gates. Blown-up photographs of notable faces are attached decoratively to a wall. These remind you, like nothing else can, not just about the talent Leicestershire once owned, but also of what it routinely lost. There is Stuart Broad, who learned his trade at Grace Road and then left to live with Notts, the more glamorous next-door neighbours. There is James Taylor, who trod the same path. Along the row is Chris Lewis too; he travelled the same route a decade before either of them. There is also Matthew Hoggard, who came to Leicestershire when Yorkshire had already benefited from the best of him. The photos tell a story that requires no interpretation. You either start your career at Leicestershire or join them in your twilight, shortly before going gently into the good night of retirement.

You never learn anything by listening to someone who agrees with your opinions. Bayliss was right to say what he thought so pointedly because it brought the debate into the open again. There are those who think his call for a cull of counties is the wisest counsel English cricket will get. The sacrifice of some branches could rescue the tree, saving us from Bayliss's 'so-so cricket' that becomes irrelevant before it perishes. But Bayliss predictably stopped short in naming the counties certain to thrive in some future Utopian summer. Possessing a ground capable of staging a Test will be the first prerequisite for survival, leaving the rest to take pot luck. The ECB would eventually have to sit in sage judgment on them; though even Solomon might feign other commitments rather than take on that job. Get rid of Gloucestershire and you lose the Cheltenham Festival. Get rid of Kent and E. W. Swanton will come back to haunt you. Get rid of Durham, already expelled from the Test arena, and first-class cricket will not travel much further north than the motorway services at Scotch Corner. I fear the eight new franchises for The Hundred – each in a big city – will be the cloak hiding the dagger, slashing at the Championship game until it contains fewer clubs, such as Leicestershire and Northampton. Say as much to the ECB and you'll get a response laced with haughty effrontery, a rebuke for the temerity of such a suggestion. They will dismiss the idea as nonsense. Their commitment to the Championship status quo will be reiterated. But, as the poet Emerson nearly said, the louder we hear them trumpeting their honour, the faster we must count the spoons.

Bayliss also didn't address the question of how – or whether – current Test players would fit in to this abbreviated Championship. Joe Root has made only nine appearances in it for Yorkshire during the past five summers. That is still one more than Ben Stokes at Durham. The carousel that is the international calendar scarcely stops whirring long enough for anyone to get off voluntarily; the demands of TV make sure of that. Even when it does slow, the likes of Root and Stokes want respite rather than a Monday-morning start at outposts such as Derby or Bristol. So the competition seldom sees the faces it most needs to give matches some attractive dressing. You can't pull in crowds without them. Of the 22 players on show at Grace Road, only one has Test experience. Northamptonshire parachuted in Doug Bracewell, owner of 27 New Zealand caps, for the push to get into Division One. Capable as Bracewell is, he will never set the turnstiles clicking.

To flourish as it should, the Championship ought to be again what it once was: the arena in which to prepare for the rigours of a Test. It can't do so because – in so far as it has one – the schedule of games makes no practical sense and merely underscores, heavily and in triplicate, the ECB's devotion to the white ball. Nothing illustrated this more than Jofra Archer's comeback from a side strain. Unfit for the first Ashes Test at Edgbaston, he needed to confirm his readiness for the second at Lord's. The last full round of Championship matches had finished in mid-July. The next full round wouldn't begin until three weeks into August. In the meantime, we were being fed an almost daily diet of Twenty20. It meant Archer had only one option open to him: a Second XI fixture between Sussex and Gloucestershire.

The Blackstone Academy Ground at Woodmancote reminded me of Sookholme, the similarities so pronounced that it was like meeting a twin. You take country back roads to reach it. One of them is so thick with trees, the high branches coiling into one another like a lovers' embrace, that it creates a dark tunnel made entirely from bark and leaves.

I stood beside the pavilion, almost identical to Welbeck Colliery's in shape and size, and admired an oak, the girth of which had 70 years' growth behind it. The distant scene was Sookholme-like too: fields abundant with crops or left fallow; electric pylons; the odd farm building or house. The Academy Ground has two pitches. The grandest of them sits on a plateau. A steward was overly concerned about drivers parking behind the pavilion. 'Do you *really* want to leave your car there?' she asked in a voice sternly serious. She imagined Gloucestershire's rookie batsmen lifting Archer straight over the pavilion's shallow roof, denting bonnets and shattering windscreens. I imagined them swaying in self-preservation.

Archer was practising his run-up and then bowling without a ball. It was a menacing-looking mime. He did some stretches. He did some 30-yard sprints, starting off like an Olympian on his blocks. He gingerly took part in a game of football, mostly avoiding the ball. The goals were small and shaped like eyelids, and Archer missed two chances, one of them an absolute howler from a yard and a half.

There are meretriciously showy sportsmen, who feel the need to tote a proscenium arch and a set of spotlights around with them. Archer isn't like that. Despite the fashion statements he makes with the gold and diamond bling of his jewellery, the moon-sized watch that is never off his wrist and his hair, clipped very artfully, he exudes self-worth and self-belief but not arrogant, chest-beating bravado. Archer knows that constant displays of brashness aren't necessary. When you can bowl at 97 mph, and do it with an effortlessly lithe and liquid grace, you don't have to go around screaming 'look at me'; you simply turn up and it happens.

I felt oddly protective towards the lads of the Gloucestershire team – seven of them teenagers – who were about to face him. There'd be no shame in mouthing 'Nearer My God to Thee' while putting the pads on and then ringing your life-insurance broker. Blackstone's is a hybrid pitch comprising 5 per cent plastic yarn woven into grass. The question was how quick Archer wanted to be on it and whether he'd be compassionate.

Archer had then played only 27 first-class matches. His last red-ball game had taken place the previous September. At 24 years old, he hasn't put roots down in the County Championship because his talent attached him instead to teams such as Rajasthan Royals, Hobart Hurricanes, Khulna Titans and Quetta Gladiators.

I found a spot on the grassy bank at the top end of the ground, which is where Archer began his opening spell. He tossed the ball up and blew on his fingers, as if to cool them down. The archetypical, snarling fast bowler pounds up to the stumps with broad shoulders and huge boots, thumping his front foot down. Think of Josh Hazlewood or – if your memory stretches further back – Colin Croft and Sylvester Clarke. Each of them could pass for heavyweight wrestlers. In civvies, Archer looks a West End dancer on a day off from burning the boards. His supple, six-foot-tall body is as slender as a jockey's whip. He moves it with loose-limbed nonchalance and a light step, half-disguising the note of combat in his stride. There is nothing over-elaborate or complicated about that gorgeous action; everything is done economically. Archer's physiology gives him the gift of speed. One of the first things you notice are his arms, longer than the ordinary mortal's, and also his hands, which are so big that he could collect half an hour's worth of rainfall in them without spilling a drop. In the well of his palm the ball looks the size of a cherry tomato. His arm, coming over, is like a catapult's release, and the wristy flick Archer gives the ball accentuates the pace and the bounce he gets. He still could do none of this without a back as strong as a coal miner's, the same attribute that made Harold Larwood so fearsome.

Before each Gloucestershire batsman took guard, there was a good deal of scratching at the crease and scanning the field. It was as though, during those extra minutes of preparation, a foolproof scheme to repel Archer would dawn on them. Of course, it never did. He bowled 12.1 overs in three spells, finishing with six for 27.

His first wicket came in his second over, taken by the wicketkeeper Joe Billings. Two more fell in the slips, one of which went so quickly there that it split the webbing of the catcher's hand. A further two were bowled, a somersaulting off stump the most spectacular of them. Another batsman perished in the covers, numbly accepting his dismissal like everyone else. Gloucestershire were never going to produce much. Being all out for 79 in an hour and a half amounted to keeping their chin just above total disaster.

Those who faced Archer possess a career highlight. It may be the most interesting thing that ever happens to them. The novices were fodder for Archer; each pinned on to the back foot in perpetual retreat. It was the safest option because he gave them approximately 0.49 seconds to decide whether to do anything else. For most of them, the bat suddenly looked a very cumbersome object indeed and the crease became the loneliest spot in sport.

Of the 73 balls Archer bowled, I estimate only two dozen thoroughly fizzed. Sweat still plastered his shirt to his back on a warm late morning. It was also an error to pick a boundary off him – even with an involuntary edge. This was like poking at a wasps' nest; for, more than likely, the punishment of a stinging bouncer or a ball that could rearrange the order of your ribs came next, a warning not to take more liberties. One of the bouncers, which the batsman mercifully dodged, went into Billings's gloves with such a smack that two birds, chirping contently in a nearby tree, flew off in startled fright as though a farmer had fired a shotgun at them.

Reg Simpson, the Nottinghamshire and England batsman of the 1940s and 1950s, used to say that there was no need for a batsman to move inelegantly when a bouncer was aimed at him. He would demonstrate his point, standing absolutely still and tracing the line of the ball with his index finger. As his finger approached the tip of his nose, he would lean back ever so slightly. 'The ball only has to miss by an inch,' he'd say. As far as I know, Simpson was never clonked on the head by a bouncer. His approach still seemed to me to be cricket's equivalent of playing chicken with a guillotine. Gloucestershire weren't prepared to take that risk against Archer.

I went to study him from the cover boundary for a couple of overs. There is a side-on photograph of almost every great fast bowler from Larwood to Trueman and from Tyson to Thomson. You look at them and think what a shame that Rodin wasn't available to chip away at a block of granite, capturing the shape of their action within it. A statue of Archer, accelerating towards the point of delivery, would be a thing of beauty.

The greatest fast bowlers, regarded with respect and envy, have qualities apart from the one everyone can see. They have an approach to battle that is just short of murderous. They are ruthlessness to the point that their hearts go out to no one but themselves. But their minds must also travel far beyond those basic instincts. Archer's does. He proved it during the World Cup final at Lord's. We coyly use words such as 'temperament' and 'mettle' in sport to euphemistically describe a performer's brass balls. Archer showed he had them in that Super Over, which he bowled so phlegmatically despite the adrenalin-quickening suspense. In the mad and improbably magnificent jumble of events, he showed something else too: the astuteness and skill to adapt and confuse New Zealand, going fuller and into the blockhole when previously he'd banged the ball in short. Even being struck for four didn't deflect him from his purpose then. Afterwards you could only wonder at the career ahead of him and the riches he would reap from it.

At the end of Gloucestershire's innings, the Sussex team stood back to allow Archer to go into the pavilion first. He was sheepish about this; after all, he'd done only what was expected of him. He gestured to a teammate and pressed his hand on to his back, walking in behind him.

On that day of delectable weather, I thought what would have happened if Archer's performance had occurred at a county ground rather than on some tucked-away field where there was no train station near by and buses passed only every hour or so. What a chance to have seen the most mesmerising new figure to have emerged during this summer. What an advertisement for the Championship. I went early to Academy Ground, not knowing how relatively remote it is; I was sure there would be a queue to watch him because of the World Cup and his imminent Test debut.

At noon, I took a head count. Only 74 of us – plus three well-behaved dogs – were relishing the spectacle of Archer running in to bowl. To everyone who wasn't there, I can only say this: you don't know what you missed.

The literature of cricket could fill an entire wing of the British Library and still require shelf space elsewhere. Among these books is a tidy collection about the creation and the evolution of the County Championship. Some are quite good, but none has been entirely successful in locking down the mood of it or the men who have most influenced the narrative of the seasons. Maybe that is because you can't just start at the beginning and carry on until you reach the end. The story of the Championship is a Hampton Court maze of a thing, impossible to tackle in a straight line. The competition is constantly changing shape in minor ways or radical ones, sending lines of history off in multiple directions – sometimes all at once.

You can even pick one of four dates for the beginning of it. The first three are 1825, 1864 and 1873. The Post Office settled on 1873, issuing stamps and a soft-backed commemorative brochure to celebrate the centenary in 1973. The stamps are line drawings of W. G. Grace, the penmanship so fluid that you think he is moving. The cover depicts Sussex versus Kent in 1849. The crowd is more interesting than the cricketers. Grand men loiter about in top hats, frock coats and long sideburns. Some of them are as stiff as corpses standing upright. Inside, you'll find the words of John Arlott: 'No other sport in the world is played, watched and recorded in detail over a seven-hour day, seven days a week for five months (of the year),' he says. The statement, factual then, was followed by something much more important: 'In terms of interest, it exerts an influence far wider and more profound than is apparent to those who have not grown up within it. To follow a county cricket team is a deeply ingrained – largely provincial – English custom, nowadays more honoured in absence than attendance.' Arlott knew it because he was a 'deeply ingrained' enthusiast himself, the boy from Basingstoke falling in love with the Championship at first sight.

We need to be kind and give Trevor Bayliss the benefit of the doubt. In being pragmatically hard-nosed about reducing the number of counties, he alighted on the probable benefits but not the probable costs. These costs would be the loss of a community institution in places which can ill afford to lose one and also a snub to a tradition that scrolls back as far as

1890, the fourth date and now accepted as the Championship's birth year.

Ever since then, the county game has seldom been a product in mass demand. The boom years have been few, but around them the Championship has generated almost too much history to consume. Even a brief summary of that past shows the agonies the competition has gone through in an effort not only to become popular, but also simply to carry on breathing. Put it this way: in the days when newspapers were produced by hot metal, the sentence that began 'There is concern for the future of the County Championship' was pre-set in a printer's block and kept handy, so frequently did it appear for one reason or another.

The game's wild schemes and wilder notions, clutched at in the hope of becoming more relevant and crowd-friendly, would stretch from one end of the St John's Wood Road to the other. Among them have been: increasing the height of the stumps . . . adding a fourth stump . . . widening the crease . . . banning left-handed batsmen (in an effort to improve the over rate) . . . amending the lbw rule . . . starting matches on different days at different times . . . playing only at weekends and over Bank Holidays . . . staging games of only one long innings . . . limiting the number of overs in the first innings to as low as 85 . . . allowing no team to bat longer than four and a half hours . . . making matches two-day affairs . . . fining teams for negative bowling . . . drawing a line across the pitch to regulate short balls.

How points were allocated, as well as the number of games each county played, has changed so often that Fermat's Last Theorem is less complicated to understand, even for the unscientific among us.

Between 1937 and 1961, four commissions were created to look into the Championship's future. There have been umpteen since. The one-day game may only have arrived just as The Beatles were warming up, but arguments about it were being traded thirty years before. In 1933 a company was created in Australia called Professional One Day Cricket Ltd.

Through all this, the smaller and less glamorous counties have always made church mice look affluent. The poor, it seems, will always be with us.

Only eight teams contested the Championship's maiden season. That total rose to nine in 1891 and to 14 four years later. Worcestershire didn't join until the end of the 19th century. Northamptonshire (1905) and Glamorgan (1921) came next. The 30th anniversary of Durham's arrival will be in 2022. Like almost everything else, the Championship emerged out of committees formed and motivated by prejudice, jealousy and self-interest. The caustic will say that we could be about to witness a repeat of it, taking us back a hundred-odd years to where we started.

I think of the prospect at Grace Road. In front of me sits a man who is recording every ball with a pencil. He has loose scorebook pages, rare these days, bulldog-clipped on to a thin piece of chipboard. If Leicestershire someday soon cease to be a first-class county, I wonder how he will spend his summers.

The crowd grows smaller as the afternoon wears slowly on and then drifts into a tranquil early evening. I go into 'The Meet', buy a cup of tea and drink it in one of the daffodil-yellow bucket seats that are stretched along the length of the boundary. I have my pick of them, able to claim an entire row to myself. I sit there in lonely isolation, like a man in an Edward Hopper painting. 'We ought to have rolled over a side as bad as this a lot sooner,' is the shouted complaint from my nearest neighbour, a Northamptonshire supporter who is at least 30 feet away. 'I won't be coming back tomorrow. Not for this.' He is agitated; it's as though his own side have inconvenienced him. Not wanting to agree or disagree, I don't turn around. Saying anything, even a sentence innocuous or platitudinous, would start a conversation that can only spin in circles. I pick up and put in the earpieces of my radio and pretend to be absorbed in the Test again, the deception a white lie. I don't even switch the radio on. The only sound I hear is bat on ball, the echo amplified in an empty ground.

The life has gone from the pitch and from Leicestershire

too. The Northamptonshire openers, already thinking of a decent night's sleep, play it safe with immaculate defence. I feel sorry for the bowlers, who have been sent into another battle that can't be won.

More people decide to go home, doing so without a second glance. Finally, even the sun turns it back on Leicestershire and leaves Grace Road.

Yet another defeat awaits them tomorrow.

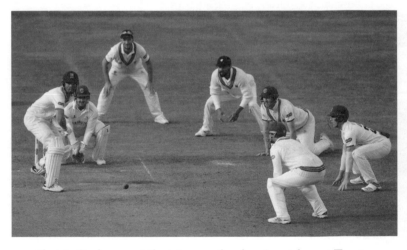

Alastair Cook, ever vigilant, ignores the close in catchers at Taunton

CHAPTER SEVEN

Shadows on the Grass

The supporter who took the early bus home. Jack Leach versus Alastair Cook. The King's England. A ground as English as high tea. Marcus Trescothick's faded maroon cap. A Poet Laureate for cricket.

He couldn't bring himself to watch another ball. The Somerset supporter, who had been sitting in front of me all afternoon, stood up in gloomy silence and looked first at the scoreboard and then at the sky, peering at them through thick-framed spectacles. Even more low cloud, gowned in black, was spreading in from the west. He tugged at the brim of his baseball cap and shook the most recent squall of rain off his maroon and white umbrella. The umbrella was pushed into a bag big enough to hold a tent. He looped the long handles of it over his right shoulder and announced. 'I'm off. See all of you next April.'

It was 2.17 p.m.. It was the last afternoon of the season's last match.

The players were walking back on to the field after briefly fleeing a hard shower that had drifted along the Bristol Channel before turning sharply right. The supporter was convinced the next of them wasn't far away.

The contest between Somerset and Essex, tantamount to a cup final, had long-since turned for him into another lament for his beloved county. On a dusty pitch, bespoke for spin, nothing much had happened very slowly. Essex, who started the weather-blighted day on 25 without loss, had moved their first innings on to 74 for one, a steady assault on Somerset's mediocre 203. They needed to do no more now than occupy the crease for a further three hours to become County Champions for the second time in three seasons. Propping up one end, Alastair Cook was turning that into a foregone conclusion.

The game, which we'd hoped would be one for the history books, had been a dud, dissolved in rain and drizzle almost since it started. Two hundred years ago this month John Keats walked out of the front door of his lodgings and returned inspired to write, enraptured, about autumn's mists and fruitfulness. He wouldn't have recognised autumn in Taunton, which seemed to have skipped straight into early winter. Only 27.5 overs were bowled on day one. Just 44.5 were possible on day two. Day three was a total washout. Today's start, at noon, was an hour and a half late. Essex contentedly gathered runs in ones and twos, minimising risk so that losing became unthinkable. With the clock against them as well as Cook, Somerset had no chance of bowling them out twice and dirt cheaply.

A boorish man, bellowing from a corner of the ground, reflected the despair without ever possessing the intelligence to know it. With no sense of the occasion and no appreciation either of the solemn effort Somerset were putting in, he offered sarcasm stripped of wit. If a shot took the edge or the bat was beaten, you would hear a burst of: 'You've got 'em, Somerset . . . They're on the run now . . . Only 19 wickets to go.' He was noisy, repetitive, predictable, tedious. Why, I thought, is there never a water cannon about when you really need one?

The neutrals, particularly those of us of a sentimental disposition, had trekked to Taunton rooting for Somerset to clinch their first title after a wait of 144 years. It wasn't that we disliked Essex or considered them villainous spoilsports for getting in the way of our wish. Our allegiance to the underdog and our romanticism just naturally carried us into the other camp. As the week passed miserably, the weather making it impossible for Somerset to control events and plot a triumph, we shared their frustration because we felt it almost as acutely. For Somerset to have again got so close to their ambition without fulfilling it seemed unfair to us and even a little gratuitously cruel.

Fate had given away the secret of the team it favoured in the third over of the final morning. Cook, on 5, was countering Jack Leach with an open-chested, two-eyed stance. He had gone back on to his stumps to defend a delivery bowled at him from around the wicket. The speed of it deceived him. So did the bounce. The ball cut back into Cook, eluded his stroke and struck him on the top roll of the pad. I was sitting in the bottom tier of the Somerset Pavilion, almost directly in line. I said instinctively and out loud: 'That's out.' I was certain of it. The umpire, Alex Wharf, didn't take long to disagree. Incredulity made Leach inarticulate, silencing every word on his lips after the initial appeal had gone aground. Cook was unconcerned. He leaned meditatively on his cream-handled Gray-Nicolls bat, the blade of which was heavily strapped near the sweet spot. You imagine it is the pose he replicates in a muddy field on his farm, a spade in his hand instead. That ball was gone and could not hurt him. He simply dedicated himself to the next.

In watching Cook take guard again, restarting his innings that afternoon, I understood why the supporter saw no point in hanging about. What he said – and something in the way he said it – told me he couldn't face the drawn-out formalities and another sorry end for Somerset. His voice was flat and dispirited. I watched his quick retreat down the steps of the stand with sympathy, never blaming him for bailing out prematurely. Your threshold for tolerating disappointment is bound to be low when you have experienced so much of it.

The supporter was of early but sprightly middle age and able to reel off, sadly by heart, not only the five seasons in which Somerset had finished second in the Championship this century, but also the circumstances behind each near miss. I suppose he was here in 2016, pacing nervously about, as Middlesex snatched the title from them after contriving a finish to beat Yorkshire at Lord's. I am guessing he saw it happen in the Stragglers' Café, the 1875 Club or the Colin Atkinson Pavilion, where club members and Somerset's team gathered together in front of a television and found comfort in commiserating with one another afterwards.

What Somerset do is never quite enough, but solace could be taken then from the fact that a conspiracy had been committed against them. The atmosphere is more maudlin this time because the blame for not winning the thing can't be apportioned elsewhere. The fault is entirely theirs. A week ago, sitting on top of the table, Somerset got messily blown to bits at Hampshire by Kyle Abbott (how long ago it seems since I saw him smash Nottinghamshire at Sookholme). Abbott took nine wickets in the first innings and eight in the second. His figures of 17 for 86 were the best in first-class cricket since Jim Laker's 19 for 90 licked the 1956 Australians at Old Trafford. While Somerset gathered up and patched together what remained of their morale at the Ageas Bowl, Essex were thumping the life out of Surrey at Chelmsford. So it was that Somerset's lead crumbled to the touch. Suddenly Essex had a 12-point jump on them.

The mathematics involved in clawing that back, daunting at the start for Somerset, had reached the impossible stage. We would have to see a comeback or a collapse so preposterously incredible that it would out-rank even Ben Stokes's heroics at Headingley. Knowing that and accepting it, the rest of us are still refusing to budge only because we don't want this – the summer of all summers – ever to end. We are going to stick it out, however banal the conclusion, until the very last ball is bowled because a whole, glum winter will separate us from the next one.

All eyes are on Cook. The writer Alan Bennett refused a knighthood because he thought 'it would be like wearing a suit all the time'. The one bestowed on Cook lies so lightly on him that you would not know he possessed it; the scorecard does not even refer to him as Sir. He brings with him an air of reliability and durability before he even faces a ball. You know, too, what you will get from him. How he will wait for the stray delivery, something short and wide-ish, that will be punched square or through the covers. How he will drive magnificently straight or sweep majestically. How, most of all, he will clip the ball solidly off his pads and past mid-wicket, the neat richness of that shot lovely to behold.

This, at 2.45 p.m., is how he reaches his 50 from a Leach full toss. It has taken him 147 deliveries and 154 minutes. Every one of those minutes merely confirmed what we knew about him: his concentration, patience and the old principles of his technique under pressure. Cook acknowledged his half-century shyly. A diffident wave of the bat is all we get in return for our applause. I thought again about the supporter who had abandoned the match. I assumed he must be nearly at his front door. I also assumed he would be listening to the radio commentary. Cook's form alone has justified his decision to take tea at home rather than here. As Cook settles back into his tall stance – Essex are now 102 for one – the only question is whether he will take a hundred off Somerset as well as the Championship pennant.

You know, unmistakably, that you've crossed into Somerset when the landscape changes so abruptly. Gradually it levels out, the countryside becoming smooth and flat as it spreads into the far distance. The tower of one ochre-stone church and then another rises beyond some high trees. The lush, empty fields suggest you could find solitude in them from the crush of the world. 'Nowhere does Somerset lose its country air,' says *The King's England*, a set of travel and topographical books that I collected second-hand as an adolescent anxious to know how the nation fitted together. On a map the coloured counties looked to me like weirdly shaped jigsaw pieces, the reason for their odd order and arrangement the most baffling conundrum. The Somerset edition of these books was first published in 1941, which explains why the text does not hold back from dwelling on old England. It describes Somerset as a county of 'romantic splendour' and 'rich in many things'. It evokes Avalon and King Arthur, the Mendip Plateau, the Quantocks, the long jaggedness of the coastline and the wide rivers and the carboniferous limestone of Cheddar, the hills honeycombed with caves. The legacy of the Roman Empire is there too, leaving the reader – then trapped in the Second World War and fearing another invasion – to draw whichever parallel pops first into the mind.

There is a sepia photograph, on page 384, looking down on Taunton's North Street. I remembered it when I arrived in the town, revelling in the luxury of solitary travel and a place I barely know. I walked along the same pavements on the way to the County Ground, the sight of the girder bridge up ahead telling me to go right before crossing The Tone and getting lost. Like every major thoroughfare in the country, North Street reminds you of the hegemony of the big shopping brands. The building that was a post office when *The King's England* went to press is nonetheless intact. So is the clock attached to it (you need a magnifying glass to spot it in the book). North Street has a pill-white post box that honours England's World Cup victory in July and also England women's World Cup win two years earlier. Since it is late September, the hanging baskets have retained their colour, but lost their bloom, and the yew tree in St James's churchyard looks as though it is already yearning for next spring.

I like Taunton. The County Ground is as English as a high tea. Stand in the gap between the Colin Atkinson Pavilion and the Andrew Caddick Pavilion and you get one of those views that, whether the sun shines on it or not, is a handsome feast. The field. The packed wooden benches of Gimblett Hill. The tower of the church climbing into the clouds behind it.

Like everywhere else, the homes of cricket change architecturally either for the purpose of improvement or out of financial necessity. I understand the motives, but can't comprehend why sometimes the development work is so uncomplimentary. A photograph taken by Patrick Eagar shows Worcestershire's New Road in 1972, a rainbow arching over both the point of the Glover's Needle and the Cathedral. Framed, signed by Eagar and hanging on my kitchen wall, I look at the picture every day and mourn the fact that some monstrosity of a hotel has since spoiled for ever that perfect view. The hotel, built on to the ground, is army-blanket grey and very flat and ugly. Putting it there was akin to sticking a multi-storey car park next to Flatford Mill. The love I had for New Road has gone cold as a consequence. Worcestershire aren't alone in allowing something unsympathetic to poke above the boundary. The flats at Bristol fall into the same depressing category. The flats at Canterbury, though not quite as horrendous aesthetically, don't really fit in either. Only at Taunton does their construction blend in so well with the scale of other structures that you aren't offended and don't necessarily notice what is there. The view is fit for the lid of a biscuit tin.

You also detect that the club and those who genuinely follow it are close kin. On Gimblett Hill I meet Harry, an eleven-year-old retriever who comes to every County Championship match and always brings his owners along with him. You don't only see dogs here. A ginger cat called Brian has staked out a half-acre of the place and claimed it as his own. I found him stretched out on a low wall, indifferent to everything except his next meal.

There is a family-like feel about Somerset and a solidarity between the members. This explains why winning the County Championship has become a matter of pride among them. You can only brood on the mystery of why it hasn't happened yet. Just as at Grace Road, the County Ground has photographs tacked to the walls that show off marquee players from Somerset's past: Cook, Langford, White, Wellard, Cartwright. So it goes on. The mystery deepens – though not necessarily in this order – when you come across the faces of Peter Roebuck, Vic Marks, Joel Garner, Ian Botham and I. V. A. Richards. Theirs was a generation so gifted, individually and collectively, that not winning the title seems – at least from a distance of thirty-odd years – more difficult than winning it. That side of all the talents proved more suited instead to lighting up Lord's in one-day finals, leaving the honour of lifting the title to those who followed them. I linger in front of one photograph in particular: Marcus Trescothick's is attached to the stand that bears his name. When I arrived at the County Ground, I chose a seat on the front row. Nowhere was more fitting. I don't mind plagiarising myself, repeating something I said a while back about Trescothick. For him not to have won a Championship seems so unjust that you want to protest and raise a petition about it.

Trescothick is 43, the accumulation of years and flesh making his 27th consecutive season his last. His debut for Somerset came in May 1993, a game here against Lancashire. That summer's film blockbuster was *Jurassic Park*, slightly ironic in retrospect because that decade as a whole seems so prehistoric to us now. When Trescothick faced his first ball in the Championship, the average price of a house was £64,000. Beer was £1.41 a pint. A train whooshed through the Channel Tunnel for the first time to test whether it was safe for travellers. That newfangled system of sending messages from one computer to another was still being referred to as 'electronic mail', a facility few possessed, fewer still understood and a lot dismissed as a passing fad. Only 11 per cent of the population owned a mobile phone.

In 391 first-class matches Trescothick scored 19,654 runs. Only 86 of those – highest score 23 – have come this season. In what turned out to be his farewell match as a batsman, facing Surrey at Guildford, he opened with his captain, Tom Abell, who was just ten months old when Trescothick announced himself on the Championship stage. Two of Somerset's other batsmen, Tom Banton and George Bartlett, were not even born. Trescothick magnanimously accepted that his career had come to a natural end. His rhythm had gone. He no longer felt 'in', he said. He didn't want to block someone else's progress. So Trescothick confronted retirement the way all his great predecessors have done since W. G., knowing the game would go on without him.

In *Cricket Country*, Edmund Blunden wrote about how all of us are the sport of Time. 'They vanish, these immortal players, and we suddenly realise with astonishment that years have passed since we last heard a mention of some of them,' he said. 'At one point they seem as much a part of the permanent scheme of things as the sun, which glows upon their familiar faces and attitudes, and the grass, which makes the background to their portrait; and then, bless us, it is time even for them to go.' The passage became more pertinent than ever when I saw eight of the 12 players who had figured in the 2005 Ashes series reunited on the outfield at Edgbaston before this season's opening Test. I looked at them and realised that 14 years had flashed by. But where? The 'boys' of that summer had become middle-aged. Some were paunchy. Some were greying. Some had lost the little hair they once possessed. I thought of Richie Benaud, commentating for the final time in England during that series. Four years have already slipped away since he died. Trescothick wasn't at Edgbaston. Nor was Andrew Flintoff, which was a bit like putting on the show without Punch. Trescothick is here, however, and being feted deservedly. Everyone wants to reminisce, shake his hand, tell him how much he is going to be missed.

Life is crammed with ifs.

If Essex hadn't beaten Surrey ... *If* Kyle Abbott hadn't rolled over Somerset ... *If* they could have brought an unassailable lead back with them to Taunton. Trescothick would then certainly have played in this game – even batting right-handed. There is another *if* too. I look at Trescothick, sitting in Somerset's Perspex dugout, and then at Cook in the middle, and think of the pair of them batting together for England. Trescothick and Cook, both born on a Christmas Day, made only seven appearances in the same Test team and never opened the innings. In 2006, against Sri Lanka at Lord's, the two of them put on 127 for the second wicket. Just as Cook got going in international cricket, so Trescothick had to give it up because of the anxiety–depression disorder he documented darkly, valuably and also bravely in his subsequent autobiography. *If* illness hadn't beaten Trescothick, you can only guess at the number of runs he and Cook would have made in tandem. Cook had 15 opening partners in Tests; Trescothick could have chopped that figure in half for him.

Two sentences finish off the paragraph from Blunden that I previously quoted. 'Cricket has its merciless side,' he adds, concluding his elegy for players with glorious careers already behind them. 'They go while they are far from being old men, and their crowded hours (or honours) are swiftly obscured in the rapid growth of new names, new methods.'

So true.

The County Ground already has a new hero. When Somerset batted and were 144 for nine, enfeebled by Simon

Harmer's spin, Jack Leach's very appearance raised flagging morale. Greeted with an ovation that would have befitted Richards at his peak, he came out practising the defensive shots that have made him a crowd darling. Grown men wore emerald-coloured T-shirts with the words NOT OUT ONE and a wagon wheel beneath of Leach's innings at Headingley.

He did what he always does. He terrorised the bowlers by frustrating them. He dobbed his first two balls to the rope at third man. The applause was loud enough to suggest we were watching one of the world's most exciting batsmen, who had barely begun to fulfil his potential, rather than the pluckiest of number elevens. Leach survived, unvanquished on 11, for 12 overs while Roelof van der Merwe played the role of Ben Stokes, biffing a 50 off 42 balls. Reporting on his role in that third Test, the *Somerset County Gazette* ran the headline: 'Leach and Stokes secure Ashes win.' As he walked off with Van der Merwe, you got the feeling his latest contribution, as far as the locals were concerned, also carried superior weight to his partner's.

Encouragement for Leach is perpetual. That boring man in the corner is confidently predicting his next success, summoning a shout of, 'Come on, Jack. You've got him now,' even when Somerset are retrieving the delivery he has just bowled from the boundary. With Cook contemplating the possibility of snatching his second hundred of the season, you hear it again as Leach is about to bowl to him. He is, admittedly, a little less vocal than before, the drop in decibel level indicative of the grim resignation of defeat that has spread across the County Ground.

Leach goes back to his mark at the River End, still chastising himself for being careless in allowing Cook those easy runs for his 50. He studies the seam of the ball, as if a fault lies in the stitching, before gripping it again between his fingers.

He turns and begins to run in . . .

Alastair Cook had been seeing it early and playing it as late as possible, allowing each ball to come to him and clearly declare its intentions. To witness him lurch forward now – a long stride of the right leg and the bat pushed slightly ahead of him – startles because it is so uncharacteristic. It's as if reaching one milestone has made him slightly giddy for the next.

Earlier in the month Cook, aware he bats with flaws as well as qualities, spoke of failure. 'You're always failing,' he said candidly of cricketers in general and specifically of himself. If he 'only' made 50, Cook felt as though he ought to have claimed a century. If he got that century, he thought he ought to have gone on to 150. Just a year ago he left Test cricket with a hundred at The Oval, satisfying those of us who dearly wanted him to depart that way. He still highlighted what the rest of us had forgotten because his feat obscured it. He had played and missed at five successive balls from Mohammed Shami. We have seen him repeatedly play and miss at Taunton too. He treats each misjudgment – outwardly at least – as nothing but the most minor of defeats. No matter how many times it occurs, he does not fundamentally doubt himself afterwards. So how do you explain what happens next against Leach?

The ball bowled is faster and flatter than the previous one. Cook is irrevocably committed to the prod. He is there too quickly and pushes at it too forcefully. The inside edge balloons off his pad, a doddle of a catch close in for Tom Banton. Cook looks mortified. On the way back to the dressing room, he slaps his bat against his leg in disgust, a small act of self-flagellation.

It is 2.48 p.m..

Leach, his tail up, reclaims the ball eagerly. We don't think anything of it. Essex will hunker down, smothering the spark Somerset have ignited before it flames. We are still thinking that way only two balls later, grossly undervaluing Leach. Dan Lawrence is bamboozled like Cook, spooning another soft catch to Craig Overton and walking off with a fat 0 beside his name. We are glad Somerset are showing fight, but are slow to realise how much of it is on display until Ravi Bopara falls to Roelof van der Merwe and the captain, Ryan ten Doeschate, is sent back too, another victim of Leach's: 102 for 1 has become 126 for 5.

We are so used to seeing Cook wear a shirt emblazoned with England's Three Lions that looking at him in county insignia, the name of a scaffolding company across his chest, seems not only incongruous but ludicrous. Then you understand that no individual in that side is more representative of the team's sponsors. Cook *is* the scaffolding around Essex. Without him, the innings looks shaky.

Tom Westley, on 36, has begun to indulge in some urgent time-wasting. He fiddles with his pads. He dithers a little before settling in his crease. He carefully pats down the pitch with his bat, as though doing so might actually make a difference to how much spin Leach can get from it. Only digging up the turf with a spade could do that now. The surface is more in cahoots with the bowlers than ever before. One over of high voltage follows another. The ball can be read out of the hand, but what it does after landing is unpredictable. The wicketkeeper, Steven Davies, takes some deliveries around his shins and bootlaces and others on or above the narrow waistband of his flannels. When Westley goes as well – snaffled in the slips – Essex are suddenly dealing with an extraordinary reversal of mood and fortune that could become a calamity.

Rain will not save them. The covers, wheeled on and off for the past 72 hours, are not needed now. The critic John Ruskin once said: 'It is a strange thing how little in general people know about the sky.' Not so with a cricket watcher. Most are as knowledgeable about all things meteorological as The Cloud Appreciation Society. The clouds visible now are high, peripheral and lamb-white. This match will end in the best weather it has known.

The previous weekend Simon Harmer, the white-ball

skipper, had come in as the 'closer', securing Twenty20 sil-verware for them by blasting a last-ball four against Worcestershire at Edgbaston. Under extreme strain – the engraver was about to inscribe a *W* on the trophy – Harmer struck his first six deliveries for 4, 1, 1, 2, 2 and 4. Here, he can't muster a scoring shot. Van der Merwe removes him for a duck, leaving Essex on 126 for seven. The last three wickets have tumbled in 11 balls.

Last season, against Lancashire, the County Ground received a final warning from the ECB's Cricket Discipline Committee – the Witchfinder Generals of pitch inspection – after a two-day finish. You begin to think whether, even if Somerset pull off this impossible mission, the ECB might descend on them again.*

The thought vanishes before it is fully formed because there is new air in Somerset's lungs, resuscitating a dead match. The Championship, like the Headingley Test, is drag-ging us to the edge of our seats when we least expected it. How tense and alive everything has become is apparent in one trivial fact. The man who couldn't stop yelling has at last fallen silent. It's as though his throat has gone dry with anxiety.

It is debatable whether Essex, Somerset or the crowd are more astonished with the last hour or so of unbelievable cricket. Somerset leap about like a team that has swallowed

---

* Somerset were subsequently docked 24 points – 12 of which were suspended for two years – because the pitch had 'excessive unevenness of bounce'. The 12-point deduction is for the 2020 County Championship season.

stimulants and are now feeling the effects of them. Essex are in shell-shocked disarray, not knowing where to turn or what to do to stop the slide. The rest of us can't look away – even to glance at one another – in case something more dramatic occurs and we miss it.

It does.

What Essex have left – Aron Nijjar, Sam Cook and Adam Wheater – succumb to Somerset's spin with minimum resistance. All out for 141, trailing by 62, Essex's last six wickets have been skittled for 15. Leach has taken five for 32. Van der Merwe has four for 41. You don't have to be a strategist like Mike Brearley, a professor of tactics, to know what Tom Abell will do. Somerset haven't left the field before Essex are beckoned back on to it; Abell has forfeited the second innings, leaving Cook to strap on the pads he took off scarcely an hour and twenty minutes ago. Someone has to calm Essex down and point out that it is 4.08 p.m.. The Championship is still theirs. Were Somerset to steal it before the close, due at 5.30 p.m., the comeback would be so unprecedented that every other in the game's history would become a footnote to it.

Word of what has already happened, along with the prospect of what could still happen, has filtered around the town in whispers and enticed in a couple of hundred stragglers. The gates are open and anyone can wander through them for free.

The latecomers aren't difficult to spot. They are unsure where to sit and immediately search for the scoreboard, afraid someone has hoodwinked them with a false rumour.

The County Ground is beautiful. A good crowd, exuberant and expectant. The clear sky an autumnal blue. Half the field in sunshine. A month from now the clocks will go back, squeezing the light out of the day, but for now the wide, long shadow cast by The Somerset Stand makes me contemplate a poem I discovered in mid-summer. Printed on the front pages of a book and originally published in *Punch*, these are the lines that grabbed me:

> *Cricket is slow*
> *Thank God for that, when fever drives the mind*
> *Let's hold this picture, though the seasons pass –*
> *The sunlit field, the shadows on the grass,*
> *And keep it slow*
> *The whole tranquil pageant in the sun*

The poem was written anonymously, but the reference to the 'sunlit field' and especially 'the shadows on the grass' could have been composed for the way Taunton looks now. It really is a picture I want to 'hold'.

I begin to think this game warrants much more than a mere scribbler for bread to write about it. I possess thick collections of cricket poetry, the bulk of them not worth the ink and paper lavished on production (John Betjeman once maladroitly rhymed Patsy Hendren with rhododendron). It is a weeping shame that no major poet – and I mean Philip Larkin during one of his ungloomy moods – was ever stirred by a match or a ground, preserving it the way Anglican churches and monuments are preserved in so much verse. Sliding on his bicycle clips, Larkin would saddle up and roam about the Yorkshire countryside in search of them. On the way, I reckon he must have passed a hundred or more cricket pitches, apparently either blind to their charms or unwilling to turn them into poetry. It is our loss. The closest Larkin came to commemorating cricket properly was a solitary line in *The Whitsun Weddings*. A game is glimpsed from the window of a passing train. He writes of it:

And somebody came up to bowl

The train rushes on, leaving us to speculate about where the ball pitched and what it did through the air afterwards (I am plumping for a delivery well up and swinging away). I suppose, if you didn't know better, you could also appropriate the last three words of that poem – 'somewhere becoming rain' – as a sly reference to cricket too.

I would have liked Larkin to become the game's laureate because cricket mattered to him and he never took it flippantly. Few know it. In *To the Sea*, Larkin remembers himself as a boy on the beach. He searches the sand 'for Famous Cricketers', which confirms his interest in them. Pretending to be a hermit in Hull, he possibly went to watch Yorkshire there. The Scarborough Festival certainly piqued his interest. 'I'm wondering if we could see any of it,' he asked his lover, Monica Jones. I like to think of him on the Popular Bank and picking up a 'pass out' at lunch, so the two of them could look down on the North Bay. Larkin also liked to watch Tests on TV. He'd switch off the sound, unable to tolerate the commentary. One of his proudest moments was becoming a member of the MCC in 1974. He boasted to his mother of strolling 'into the pavilion wearing my bold red and yellow tie'.

If only Larkin was here now.

The County Championship has made every Somerset captain look like Ahab chasing the whale. Last night I went into the Nando's on North Street and found myself queuing to order in front of Tom Abell, the latest of them. Two of his friends, a father with a young son, joined the queue behind me. 'What do you think about our prospects, then?' the father asked. Abell turned, folded his arms and replied, 'Well, 20 wickets in a day. With us, you never know.' He went no further, perhaps tethering to reality the unspoken thought that came next. During the pause, which Abell left before switching the subject, I wanted to tell him I'd been at Headingley and that 'anything was possible'. I was on the verge of saying so when I realised how stupidly superfluous it would be; he could glean that information from the expert in his own dressing room.

Now Abell has sixty-seven minutes to magic something up through the sheer force of his optimism. He waves his fielders around the bat, creating a cul-de-sac of them.

The minor mess Essex have got themselves into gives us the pleasure of Alastair Cook again. He was nudging 34 when he quit England. Someone used to the swanky high life – Melbourne on Boxing Day or Lord's on a June Saturday – could have said that a damp morning at Chelmsford no longer appealed to him. Everyone would have understood and been uncritical of his decision to retire. Cook, conscious of the pleasure cricket has given him, opted to go through the slog again. His last full Championship season was in 2005. He made 1,249 runs. His half-century here took him to 883 runs for this season. His average is 40-plus. It isn't bad because big scores have not been particularly plentiful anywhere in such a disjointed competition. He has also been facing bowlers he knows well and others he knows hardly or not at all.

To have even a squeak of pulling off an upset, Somerset must take a shower of wickets quickly. The most precious is Cook's, but the former England captain has played so long and seen so much. He isn't burdened by the responsibility on him now. As good as it is – which is very good, sometimes – the Somerset attack of Jack Leach, Roelof van der Merwe and Dom Bess also counts as everyday compared to some of the top-notch bowling Cook made his living against in Tests. He can't be ensnared. Leach may as well be practising against the outside wall of the County Ground; nothing significant gets past Cook's bat and no chance is given.

The only quirk about him is his running. Even when taking an easy single, Cook often dashes to safety like someone late for the last train. He is so jerky in his long-limbed movements that his joints look ready for a drop of oil. As if to avoid the bother of stretching those spindly legs, he goes back on to his stumps and pushes a four casually off Leach instead. He drives another against him, the over-pitched delivery dispatched exquisitely. He powerfully pulls two short balls from Van der Merwe to the boundary too. The scoreboard ticks over and the clock ticks on. Essex draw deep, calming breaths of relief.

It is 5 p.m..

Somerset finally take a wicket; Cook's partner, Nick Browne, goes when the score is 38 in the 17th over. By then, only the motions are to be gone through.

I watch the last rites with a friend. Like Cook and Marcus Trescothick, we were born on the same day at Christmastime. Unlike them, only a few hours, rather than a lot of years, separate our births. We saw Cook masterfully take charge, moving untroubled on to 30. We saw Trescothick's cameo appearance as a substitute fielder – part of it spent on his knees as a close catcher, a supplicant in a hopeless cause. The cap he wore was so faded that it could have been the first Somerset had ever given him. What a privilege, I thought, to witness all this; for it is terribly rare indeed to be there when a consummate cricketer, who is also a man of enviable substance, takes his curtain call. Trescothick received one standing ovation as he came on to the pitch and another with a guard of honour as he left it. Only the trimmings – a red carpet and a brass band – were missing. We would have begrudged him neither.

It is possible to go looking for one thing and discover another. I came to see Somerset win the title. What I found was even better than that.

My friend and I began taking backward glances over travelled roads. As the game dawdled to its finish, we talked affectionately about decades-old matches we'd seen, the players we most admired and some of the performances that had defined them. In these shared memories, the obscure – once cult figures in the county game but forgotten now – got equal billing alongside the famous. To an eavesdropper, I suppose we must have sounded like a combination of Francis Thompson recalling his Hornby and his Barlow of 'long ago', ghosts all about us, and Henry Newbolt caught in the 'breathless hush of the close'. As we traded tales, it seemed to me that one blissful year was linked indistinguishably with the next.

My whole cricket-watching life became one long and beautiful summer.

The afternoon we were enjoying invited that sort of reflection because it chimed so sweetly with our ideal of the County Championship and reinforced our love for it. Wildly unpredictable almost to the last, the game had gripped and then dazzled us. Somerset and Essex had shown how much the title mattered to both of them. And everything about the gentle end, at 5.20 p.m., was absolutely perfect, revealing as it did the sporting civility of victor and vanquished alike and also the camaraderie among cricketers who began this quest in the cold weeks of April when the air was like iron and pitches were like dough.

The Championship was settled with the handshake that Abell offered and Cook accepted readily. He had faced 48 of the 108 balls bowled. Essex, on 46 for 1, needed only another 18 to win. An avaricious side, wanting to rub in their superiority, would have gone for it, slogging everywhere with impunity for the last ten minutes. A draw, though, was not only just but also respectful in the circumstances and a showcase of grace and humility too; I felt proud of the spirit of Championship cricket.

We knew Essex, topping the table by 11 points, were worthy Champions, indisputably the best and the brightest. The team had brushed off a bad defeat in its opening game and galloped on to nine wins and four draws, a sequence that included the 151-run crushing of Somerset at Chelmsford in June. Simon Harmer had claimed 83 wickets. Cook was only 87 short of 1,000 runs. Westley, Lawrence, Porter and Peter Siddle, prior to his Ashes duties, did more than chip in beside them.

I stay for the presentation. Most of it is inaudible, staged thoughtlessly for the purposes of the television viewer on the sofa rather than for the paying customer behind the fence.

The toughest thing about success is that you have to go on

being successful. But as Ryan ten Doeschate raises the gold trophy, and risks being drowned in Veuve Clicquot, I ponder only on who can possibly beat them to another title next summer. If anyone does, I'd like it to be Somerset, of course.

And so the season falls into silence.

I sit quietly on Gimblett Hill for a while and gaze across a field almost wholly swallowed by shadow. The scene is serene but also desolately sad. The story of the match has been wiped clean from the scoreboard. The sun has gone in, the chalice in Ten Doeschate's hands glimmering beneath the floodlights. He and his side gradually become indistinct in the twilight. Eventually I see only the odd blur of white clothing on the balcony of their dressing room.

In that wondrous but illogical way that memory has of digging up something half-forgotten and suddenly flashing it in front of your eyes again, I start to remember the last match of a season at Trent Bridge. I am walking slowly down the pavilion steps. I open the pavilion gate and then ceremoniously close it behind me. The click of the latch formally marks the end of summer. I follow the curve of the boundary rope as far as the Radcliffe Road end of the ground before slipping between a gap in the advertising boards and turning reluctantly for home. I had the consolation of knowing then that the following season would be shaped like all the previous ones. Now, with a sleepy winter to come, I want to cling on tight to the last six months because it feels as though I may not experience anything like them again.

An era seems to have ended. If so, at least I saw some of it.

The landmark every cricket devotee recognises.

Behind the Scenes at the Museum

Fielding at leg slip in 1906. A giant once lived here. An
ageing relative, barely kept alive. A door into the past.
Bloody carnage on the coast. The aesthetics of cricket.

The sky in south London is so grey and so flat that it looks as
though someone has shaded it in with the heaviest of HB
pencils. The dark pavements glisten with early morning rain,
the last of autumn's bedraggled leaves sticking to them and
making each slab slippery underfoot.

I am, as always, embarrassed to be so absurdly early for an
appointment, which today is a tour of The Oval. I idle away
three quarters of an hour or more, dawdling around the outside of the ground. I stop on the corner of Clayton Road and
stare at the high rim of the gasometer, thinking that nowadays

it could almost pass for a piece of minimalist installation art and win a prize. I look at the decrepit, peeling signage and also the boarded-up windows of The Cricketers, remembering the beery warmth once trapped behind them. On the pub forecourt, where unruly tufts of grass are sprouting, a jackdaw is pecking furiously at a white plastic bag; his squabble with the bag ends only when he flees with it into the topmost branch of a tree.

At one of The Oval's gates, it's possible to peer through the narrow black railings and glimpse a tantalising flash of greenery. Beyond the empty, sodden outfield is the scoreboard, awaiting the feats of next summer. Beyond that is the sturdy red brick of Archbishop Tenison's School Academy. Near by, there is the growl of a bulldozer making hills out of dusty rubble, and the gear-grinding screech of a small crane, which rearranges the debris more neatly. As a constantly progressive county, Surrey epitomises the belief that everything will retrograde if it does not advance. The Lock and Laker Stand, beside the pavilion, is being demolished so it can be rebuilt and enlarged.

I like The Oval. I like walking out of the Tube and finding the classical Grecian façade and pillars of St Mark's Church to my right and the Hobbs Gate, as unpretentious as the man himself, to my left. I also like the fact that the newspaper stall on Harleyford Street always reminds me of John Arlott's article about his friend 'Smithy' at Headingley; 37 different newspapers are spread across a wooden trestle table. I could half-convince myself that the printed word is thriving.

I am here in late November because something deeply ironic struck me during the season. I suppose it began at Lord's.

At the end of July, on a day almost equidistant between the World Cup final and the opening Ashes Test, I had gone there with a friend, who is a member of the MCC. I was startled to walk through the gates unchallenged. Lord's was still and very silent. The pitch on the Nursery End ground was covered. On the main square, one groundsman walked up and down staring hard at each strip. Another groundsman was cutting the outfield in front of the Grandstand, the phut-phut of the mower the only sound to be heard. Early afternoon sun glinted off the Media Centre. We headed for the Pavilion. The steward on the door gave a deferential nod to my friend, standing aside and gesturing us in. It felt as if I was sneaking into a grand country house when the owners were away on holiday. I took in the scent of new polish and old dust and the squeak of the floorboards. At the top of stairs, on the way into the Long Room, we found both the portrait of Viv Richards and Albert Chevallier Tayler's *Kent versus Lancashire at Canterbury in 1906*, the cricket painting I would most like to steal for that spot above the mantelpiece. The canvas was hung, completely inappropriately, at the same height that Chevallier Tayler would have placed it on his studio easel. Standing in front of it, my friend and I could kid ourselves that Colin Blythe had waved us inside the frame and asked us to field at leg slip.

We lingered there for a while, thinking of the smart catches we'd have definitely taken, before leaving Blythe to bowl to J. T. Tyldesley, as he always will. We went next door, where high windows brought in great washes of light. My friend pointed at the opposite wall. A painting showed a gaggle of barefooted Victorian boys. None of them must have owned a coin; a bat, spun into the air, was being used for the toss. I looked at the Pavilion benches, imagining the hierarchical jostling that must go on – formally or informally – to settle who sits where. I decided the MCC's gentry are rather like those bigwig families who command the front pews of their local church.

The thought I had at Lord's returned to me at Hove and then again at Taunton. At Hove, it was because I saw C. B. Fry's sweater. Age had frayed the cuffs and the straggly hem, but the sweater was wide enough around the chest and the shoulders for two men to fit inside it without having the breath squeezed out of them. An entire flock of sheep must have been shorn to produce that much wool. At Taunton, it was because I came across the bat Bill Alley used in 1961 when, aged 42, he became the last man in England to score 3,000 runs in a season. In one match Alley made 221 not out in Somerset's total of 311. The size of the bat amazed me in the same way that the size of Fry's sweater had done – but for a different reason, obviously. The thing was such an insubstantially thin piece of wood that no one nowadays would wield it in a game of beach cricket.

Edward Thomas said that the past is the only dead thing that smells sweet. As I travelled from ground to ground, it became apparent how much the counties have become aware of that – and aware also of their responsibility to seek out and preserve history. Following where Lord's has so splendidly led, collecting and displaying cricketana, corners of long rooms or pavilions have been set aside or even separate museums created so the game's artefacts can be protected under glass.

This deferential respect towards cricket's heritage is relatively new. Look back at the small ads that appeared in *Playfair Cricket Monthly* less than half a century ago and you'll occasionally find for sale what would now be considered as valuable treasure. You could buy for a cheap song one of A. E. Stoddart's bats or a signed menu card from the 1936–7 Ashes tour, an MCC cap that Sir Pelham Warner wore or a ball Wally Hammond bashed for a six. You could acquire, for comparatively next to nothing, a lot of Bradman memorabilia too.

Now counties actively seek possession of what once only sat on top of the sideboards or in the cabinets of private collectors. For them no trinket is too trivial to be shelved or catalogued. Bats and pads and gloves. Scorecards and snuff boxes and cigarette cases. China figurines and ceramic pots and enamel badges. Prints, paintings and aquatints. Match tickets and posters, letters and other printed ephemera of all sorts. The counties preserve the inanimate, hoping something of a long-ago yesterday will still physically exist in it for us.

The thing about an obsession is that it never ends. So I have to confess this: I can never satisfactorily scratch the nerdy itch of my curiosity.

It is never the gold or the silverware, the elaborately engraved cups and bowls and medals, or even the record-breaking bats that appeal to me. The everyday and the ordinary, the sort of personal bric-a-brac that passes through all our hands, is always far more fascinating. A black fountain pen with a gold nib that Douglas Jardine owned. A pair of spectacles and a box of matches belonging to Percy Fender. A two-paragraph thank-you letter Wilfred Rhodes wrote on Yorkshire's headed notepaper. The tortoiseshell-coloured comb that Denis Compton swept through his slickly Bryl-creemed hair. The trivially private items peculiarly make me feel a little connected to whoever owned them. A cigarette case (Arthur Carr's). A pipe, the stem chewed (Fred True-man's). A scrapbook, the cuttings in it immaculately arranged (Len Hutton). A capacious trunk with MCC insignia that once crossed the oceans for an Ashes tour in Australia (Godfrey Evans). These are the pieces I seek out, ignoring the grander stuff.

There is only one county museum that I haven't stepped inside.

★

For those of us who appreciate what the counties are doing, it's a solace to see them holding on to a past that is fast receding. But it also brings more sharply into focus what cricket could be about to give up and the probable ramifications of that.

I realise it again at The Oval.

In April, the wealthiest and arguably the most influential county reported pre-tax profits for a ninth successive year: £2.7 million on a turnover of £31.7 million. Surrey have strung up banners that proclaim The Oval as 'THE HOME OF TWENTY20', justifying the claim with their accounts (you can almost hear Warwickshire harrumphing their objections). Last season's seven games here were watched by a total crowd of 170,000. Each game netted about £1 million in revenue.

Surrey didn't only resist The Hundred and question with scepticism the figures, the logistics and the strategy the ECB presented about it. They also voted against the launch, the only county to do so. The friction between them and the ECB, who dislike dissent, generated sufficient attritional heat at one stage to have started a bonfire. Surrey felt, as most of us do, that jamming the untried new format between the existing ones threatened to disrupt next summer and eventually corrode those to come. The ECB offered only a marketing survey to proclaim The Hundred's viability. Surrey laid down, with the flourish of a trump card, the concrete evidence of their balance sheet to explain why there is no need for it. Surrey think the £180 million or so the ECB will lavish on The Hundred during the next five years could be more sensibly lavished on Twenty20 instead. Indeed, if the ECB had peddled Twenty20 to a terrestrial broadcaster, The Hundred would never have been conceived.

With all this cash coming in, Surrey have made The Oval a 21st-century ground. It reminds me of Harold Macmillan's remark about the House of Lord's: 'Such a wonderful place for an old man. You cannot walk twenty yards without finding a bar or a lavatory.' At the same time, however, the club has been magnificently celebrating the fact that its origins are in the 19th century. The ancient and the modern rub elbows with one another.

You are always coming across an oak honours' board or a plaque that marks the Tests staged here, the records established during them or an individual's landmark performance, such as Len Hutton's indefatigable innings against Australia in 1938. Of course, Surrey's County Championships – 19 of them – appear in gold lettering too. The Pavilion doesn't need wallpaper. The corridors and passageways are covered in framed blazers, paintings, photographs, letters, posters and match bills. There are etchings and aquatint prints of The Oval, predating the construction of the gasometer. Follow them chronologically and you'll see the ground, once no more than a patch of reasonably well-rolled grass, grow impressively around you. No one makes this much fastidious effort without caring profoundly about the importance of tradition, the evolution of the game and the lineage of those who have played it.

The Oval's museum and library is like one of those antique shops in which you want to look at everything at once but don't know where to start. At first, you can't take it all in. The most recent acquisition is a silver teapot with a stubby spout, the sort your grandmother or great-grandmother would have displayed prominently in her china cabinet as a family heirloom. The teapot was presented to Jack Hobbs's opening partner, Andy Sandham, after he got a big score in Tasmania. The mundane is about to be given its beautiful due – polished, labelled, put on a shelf. The most modern exhibit – apart from Ben Stokes's just-published book about his summer heroics – is the pair of gloves Alastair Cook wore in his last Test. He signed and donated them.

My eyes dart elsewhere. In a low glass case are a pair of Alec Bedser's bowling boots. I can't stop looking at them.

Hanging in the Long Room you'll find a double portrait of Bedser and his twin and teammate, Eric. The artist, June Mendoza, painted the bachelors at home. The licence she took is ingenious. The Bedsers lived together near Woking, but the view Mendoza depicts through their lounge window is of The Oval and the gasometer, stressing where their love and loyalty lay.

Bedser's boots are size 15. It's as though a giant has left them behind. Bedser was actually no taller than six foot, but I remember, from the only time we ever met, that he was as broad as an Edwardian wardrobe and his hands were as huge as a ditchdigger's shovel. The toecaps on the boots could kick down a bank door. The spiked soles are dark brown and look cardboard-thin. Bedser's feet were surely the colour of tenderised beef after wearing them during long spells on hard pitches. The leather, once white, is fawn-coloured. I count nine lace holes, which would have enabled Bedser to strap himself into them. The tops of the boots stretched high over his ankles, supporting the joints. I look at the creases on the instep and also at the ragged heel. At the end of a day's play, he must have yanked off the boots with his thumbs.

Bedser, born in 1918, fought in the Second World War, a campaign which began for him with evacuation from Dunkirk. Delivering the ball at 'something above medium pace', his career, which brought him 1,924 first-class wickets (and also 236 in 51 Tests), consequently didn't hit full steam until 1946. When it did, Bedser toiled harder than Boxer in *Animal Farm*. He played 485 first-class matches, took 100 wickets in a season 11 times and retired at 42. You can extrapolate about how astonishingly successful Bedser would have been if he hadn't spent six years of his healthy 20s in khaki. In Coronation year alone he sent down 1,253 overs, taking 162 wickets. I wonder how he was still able to stand up in September. Compare that Surrey summer to the one just gone. Morne Morkel bowled the most Championship overs for the club: 413.

I hadn't expected to find Bedser's boots. When I do, I am

surprised to be slightly moved by the intimate sight of them. Often it's said that to understand someone you have to imagine yourself walking in their shoes for a mile. I imagine Bedser on the field here, which the window of the museum overlooks, bowling until he almost dropped. His boots revealed the essence of his character, the cricketer as a working man.

When Bedser died, aged 91 in 2010, the obituaries gave the impression that he had been exceptionally old school. His personality determined the kind of player he became; no-nonsense-tough, unfancy, uncomplicated. He retained 'a steadfast affection for the Championship'. Experiments and restructuring were 'anathema to him'. He was 'suspicious' of 'the surfeit of fixtures and competitions' too.

As I stare at these dead man's boots, taking a photograph in case no one believes my description of them, the ironic thing that first occurred to me at Lord's returns even more forcefully than before. The counties, at last fully committed to cricket's history, are accumulating souvenirs so prolifically at the very point at which few may be interested in them.

If The Hundred alters every summer, making it almost unrecognisable to us, these old fragments and trophies will not mean much – if anything at all – to the new audience cricket attracts. Those who watch won't be weighed down by history or memory. For if neither Tests nor the County Championship appealed to them in the first place, why would the relics of long-ago matches? You have to know who Bedser was, and what he did, to be interested in his belongings or what he wore. You have to care as much about where cricket came from as where it might go. And you have to be aware of how the game has been steadily shaped; otherwise the objects you're looking at will have little relevance to you and no context either. It would be like going blindly into the Ashmolean and being unable to tell the difference between what is Greek and what is Roman and not knowing either why that matters.

The thought tinges everything about my visit with a little sadness.

I stand for a while looking at a sign that is nailed to a wall. THE BRADMAN DOOR, it says. The door itself is very ordinary; just plain wood and a panel of glass. In 1948 Donald Bradman walked beneath the lintel of it for his final Test innings, returning two balls later with the most notable duck in history. It proved Bradman could be famous even for his failures.

In retrospect you can always find curious connections, unapparent to you when they occurred. The door reminds me that the Ashes series of 1948 – and specifically Bradman and Arthur Morris – seems to have been following me around for most of the summer.

On my way home from Taunton, I began talking to an elderly gent at the railway station. He had a ticket for the London train, which was already half an hour late. We quickly established that we'd both spent the day watching Alastair Cook win the County Championship. I assumed, given the destination of his train, that he was travelling victoriously back to Essex. 'Oh no,' he said. 'I'm a Somerset man. Jack Leach is my nephew.' We spoke for a while about Leach's boyhood, his development as a cricketer and his Bailey-like blocking in the Headingley Test. We talked about the future of the Championship, singing the same hymns about it. Somehow, we got on to some of the earliest cricket he had watched. 'I saw the '48 Invincibles,' he said. 'A friend even gave me a bat signed by the team. I eventually gave it back. I thought it wasn't fair that I clung on to something so precious, which wasn't really mine.' I asked how his friend had come to own it. 'Arthur Morris got it for him,' he said. I was about to mention my meeting with Morris. I also wanted to tell him my favourite anecdote about the 1948 tour, thinking it related perfectly to our conversation about the Championship. His train came whistling in just as I began to speak; only a few words of the sentence spluttered out.

The Bradman Door brings back what I was going to say to him. It was this.

One bright Whitsuntide Saturday in 1948, a man decided to take the first great love of his life to gaze at his second. On holiday from the Isle of Wight, he persuaded his fiancée, who was called Audrey, to watch cricket, a game which she'd never sat through before and apparently showed scant interest in. Australia were playing Essex at Southend, the tourists' sixth match of what would become their Invincible Summer. The couple were among a crowd of 16,000.

With its trees, tents and smart pavilion, Southchurch Park looked too quaint a place for absolute carnage, but what occurred there can't be described as anything else. In fact, digging out every synonym of that word and writing each one beside it would still only partly convey how ruthlessly Essex were chopped into a bloody heap. Even now, so long after the event, the raw statistics make your eyes pop a little with incredulity when you stare at them. In 350 minutes, Australia scored 721 runs at a rate of 5.59 per over. No team in England had ever made so high a total in a single day. Donald Bradman, three months shy of his 40th birthday, was on his farewell lap of honour around England. He hit 187, an innings including 32 of the 87 boundaries taken off a feebly inadequate attack. His century came in less than an hour and a quarter. He scored the rest of his runs in only 48 minutes.

Essex's bowling figures were a casualty list. Eric Price, the left-arm spinner, was bashed for 156 runs from 20 overs; he didn't get a sniff of a wicket. The hand that finally bowled Bradman belonged to the leggie Peter Smith, who at least had a story to pass on to his grandchildren – even though he possibly glossed over the 193 runs he conceded.

Not everyone was impressed with the whirlwind that Australia whipped up on that May day. 'The afternoon sun was not long on its downward path before boundaries were received in complete silence,' wrote Jack Fingleton, gloomily. He believed that the 'spectators had had too much of a good thing', the parade of fine shots becoming monotonous to them. One alternative explanation is that their hands were sore from clapping and their voices had dissolved in whispers from over-acclaiming the feast in front of them. Another is that Fingleton himself was bone-weary of a battle in which one side could do nothing more than retreat and tend to the wounded. He failed to notice that everyone else around him was simply stupefied rather than bored.

The man who took his fiancée to the game certainly sounded as though he'd felt that way. His name was Kenneth Hoskins. Four decades after the event, he wrote to *The Cricketer* about it. I found his letter many years ago in a bound copy of the magazine. I hadn't come across his piece of 'I Was There' history before and I have never seen it since. I felt as if I'd dug up a small gold coin in a hundred-acre field of archived print. I don't know what drew me to that particular corner of that particular magazine – serendipity is all I can offer – but I caught the gleam of what was there from the first line. The anecdote illuminated the match for me much more than any contemporary newspaper report had ever done. I instantly pictured Mr Hoskins and Audrey. I put him in a sports jacket and a pair of slacks, his dark hair slicked back and his white shirt open at the neck. I decided Audrey was a blonde in a polka-dot dress. She wore pale red lipstick and white sandals. I confess that in thinking of her, I couldn't shake off Bert Hardy's well-known photograph of the girl sitting on the railings at Blackpool. One became quite indivisible from the other for me.

I went as far as imagining how the conversation between them must have gone during the build-up to the match and the eager big sell he'd given Audrey to clinch the date. He'd have filled in the background for her, going on about the phenomenon that was Bradman and how he wouldn't be passing that way again. He'd have talked about other matches he'd seen and also the players who had flashed through them. I suspected her of feigning some gripping interest and even humouring him, asking a few perfunctory questions before pretending to care about the answers.

The game she saw was staggering then and more so in retrospect. Southchurch Park isn't The Oval, where the outfield is the size of a country park, but it must have taken a lot of time to retrieve the ball from the boundary and hurl it back to the bowler. Yet Essex still managed to get through 129 overs. The surprise is that, despite the pummelling the Australians gave them, no one attempted to slow down the rate, taking ponderous and deliberate stock of a dire situation. Or micro-manage the field placings. Or ask for one drinks break after another. Or protest that Bradman had battered the ball out of shape. What you got, from late morning until early evening, was perpetual entertainment. At the end, rather than turn and go home, the crowd came over the fence. The field disappeared beneath people. The few police among them had to force a path for the players from pitch to pavilion, a piece of evidence that doesn't fit at all with Fingleton's claim about yawning indifference towards the slaughter.

I once toured the wooden scoreboard at The Adelaide Oval, a construction first used in 1911 and spread over four storeys. The thing is a historical monument. These days you have to be wary about using the word 'iconic' because it routinely gets attached to almost everything built barely a fortnight ago, making nonsense of the dictionary definition. But this scoreboard is iconic. Pull it down, as some heretics have suggested, and you'd be guilty of desecration.

I saw it on a hot, shiny morning in the City of Churches. Inside the scoreboard, each floor cool and dim, you viewed the ground through what is best described as a square porthole. The simplicity of the exterior hid a contraption of Heath Robinson complexity. The knowledgeable guide, who knew every nook in it, talked about wheels and pulleys, handles and shutters, ropes and cogs. You needed a staff of six to work it during a match, he said.

I thought about the scoreboard operators at Southend. There were only two of them, stuck in what amounted to not much more than a shoebox turned on one end. Essex hadn't conceived that a total of 700 was ever possible and so made no preparation for it. They ran out of the number 7. The operators, flummoxed in the beginning and then panicky, weren't fast enough to keep pace with the rate of scoring. They flung themselves about like wasps trapped in a jar. The scorers were similarly flustered, having to sharpen and re-sharpen their pencils.

Those who saw the game boasted about it. Those who hadn't simply pretended to have been there, more than trebling the gate, and convinced themselves it was true. At least one person, who could brandish her ticket as proof of her presence, saw the day differently from everyone else. For posterity's sake, Mr Hoskins recorded the exchange Audrey had with her uncle, who was giving them bed and board that weekend.

> 'Well, Audrey. What did you think of that for first-class cricket?' he asked her.
> 'It's all right, I suppose,' she replied, 'but a bit slow.'

I always wonder how many more games Audrey saw. Perhaps, on another Whit Monday, she sat through a match in which fewer than 250 runs were scored. How slow would *that* amble have seemed to her.

I couldn't let the story go. I had to find out what happened to the couple. Reader, the remarkable thing I discovered is this: however bored Audrey must have been without showing it, she married Kenneth the following year. If Bradman had known, he would surely have sent a telegram of congratulation.

It has to be said that *The Cricketer* underplayed the 40-year-old scoop, sticking it between a toast to R. M. Poore's career and a complaint that Lancashire's 'Flat' Jack Simmons hadn't been chosen for a Test against the West Indies. What

The Cricketer missed was this. In her polite way, Audrey articulated the problem cricket has always faced when trying to
expand and become more popular. The punchline to the letter,
which was the whole reason for writing it, makes the story
instructive, a moral for the game.

There are people who are simply never going to get cricket,
which demands patience, rigour and concentration. A special-
ised taste, it will always be too slow for some – however much
it changes and however fast it accelerates to achieve a result,
purely to satisfy the impatient among us.

I sat on the dimpled green leather benches that run along
the committee room balcony at The Oval. The sun briefly
came out. It was too fragile to stay or to warm anything.
The stands were bare except for a man in black overalls who
was briskly sweeping one of the aisles. The empty field, after
recent weeks of bad weather, looked princely and dignified
nonetheless. Even on this dank day it offered a sustained
intensity of colour. With as much modern pomp as the ECB
can muster, the opening match of The Hundred will be
staged here. It will offer Surrey the chance to put up another
commemorative plaque afterwards – if the club can find the
wall space.

The benches offer a box seat, the best and most comfortable
view in the whole ground. I could see the misty outline of the
Palace of Westminster and the huge blanched-white wheel of

the London Eye, turning as slowly as a clock. Cardinal points of the capital poked above a fuzzy, blue–grey haze that was coiling across the rooftops from the unseen Thames.

In The Oval's library, a small room next to the main body of the museum, I had searched for – and could not find – a copy of Edmund Blunden's *Cricket Country*. I had been right: no one had noticed the landmark anniversary of its publication. Instead I discovered Neville Cardus's *The Summer Game*, a favourite of mine and of Blunden's too. I turned a few pages randomly. In the title essay I came across this: 'It is the brevity of a cricket season that makes the game precious,' says Cardus. Alone, and sitting on those green benches, I contemplated what made it particularly precious to me.

I was attracted to cricket because I saw something greater in it than the thing itself. The game has always been a big part of my life because, paradoxically, it makes me happy in a lot of small ways.

Cardus, the father of literate sports writing, felt the same way. He once wrote that if a psychoanalyst was to engage him in a word-association test, his response to 'Cricket' would include the following: 'Lord's . . . buckle missing on pad . . . next man in . . . shady pavilion with shirts on pegs all inside out . . . a new bat and linseed oil'. My own list would comprise: scorebook and pencil . . . the toss of the coin . . . the clang of the bell that brings the umpires on to the field . . . a church spire rising above some trees . . . a lawnmower travelling gently across the outfield . . . afternoon tea and wicker picnic baskets . . . the sound you hear when the sweet spot of the bat greets the ball . . . the sight of that ball hitting the rope and then bunny-hopping over it . . . a match found serendipitously on some village green unfamiliar to me.

I have something else in common with Cardus. The aesthetics of cricket – the fluidity of a bowler's action or a gracefully flashing stroke – have always mattered more to me than the statistics of it. The record books I own sit obscurely on a bottom shelf. Some of them are smothered in a decade of undisturbed dust. Had I been at Southend, for example, I'd have been bewitched by the easy manner in which Donald Bradman got his runs before bothering to look at the number he'd accumulated.

Cardus was a garrulous man; some university ought to have bestowed on him an honorary degree in talking. He could go on lyrically and for ever about Spooner and Parkin, Compton and Constantine, Verity and Larwood. The poet in him was stirred because each showed themselves capable of summoning performances of seductive glamour. Cardus, bored easily, craved a demonstration of style irrespective of substance. He also wanted more than even the finest could give him. It tells you why, just occasionally, he strived for the emotional truth rather than the literal truth in his writing. But adapting Ruskin's argument, which is about a single room of Turner landscapes being worth an entire gallery of anyone else's, I would never be without my library of his work.

He was a Victorian who lived long enough to see the birth and the infancy of the one-day game. It disturbed him. The scores were paltry by today's standards; 250 in 65 overs was considered whiz-bang scoring. Cardus still forecast what was coming: the County Championship gradually shrinking over time in size and status. In the early 1970s, which were Cardus's final years, a batsman really had to middle a shot to make it soar. Clearing a Test boundary was rare enough to guarantee you a generous, astonished mention in dispatches the next morning. Cardus found the thump of sixes repetitively monotonous. If belting a six became commonplace, he said, you would cease to be amazed at the spectacle and groan disappointedly when it didn't happen.

In hindsight, Cardus might have concentrated on the positives of the Championship instead of the negatives of the one-day game. He was an expert on it, the only writer still breathing who had seen matches in both the Golden and Silver Ages*. For a lot of people, the definition of history is the time just before they were born. For Cardus, it stretched further back than the day Broadhalfpenny Down was first seeded and watered. Whatever he said about the Championship couldn't have been airily ignored; whereas his chiding of the one-day stuff could be – and usually was – dismissed as the dyspepsia of a grumpy old git stuck in the sludge of the past. This is more than a pity. The

---

* E W Swanton, born in 1907, is supposed to have watched W G Grace 'from my perambulator' in 1910, but that hardly seems to count.

Championship needed – and still needs – the most eloquent advocates it can find.

The more I thought of Cardus, the more one sentence came to mind – the most evocative he ever wrote because it catches so much light.

I am often considered to be ever so slightly dotty for not wanting to leave England during the cricket season and also for choosing holiday spots which have a first-class cricket ground reasonably close by. I don't care. I believe England would look a little bare without the decoration cricket brings to the landscape between early April and late September. I also believe something goes out of the year – and so out of England too – when the season is over. I am left longing for the next. No one else has distilled those feelings into prose like Cardus, who did it in a single line.

There can be no summer in this land without cricket.

It was mid-afternoon when I got up from the committee benches and left The Oval. The sky was even darker than before, the clouds about to close out the day. A small wind came up, strong enough to lift even some of the wettest leaves off the pavement. I felt the surroundings very acutely because the old season seemed long past and the new one felt far away. In this limbo, I walked out of the Hobbs Gate, glancing only briefly back at the hulking Pavilion. I clung to those ten words of Cardus's, a comfort against what may or may not happen to the game in the very near future; for they always remind me of three things.

How blessed I am to have been born here. How I never want to live anywhere else. How much I love cricket.

Author's Notes and Acknowledgements

On page 42 of *One Long and Beautiful Summer*, I make the following point: 'It may seem trite and somewhat out of proportion to invoke *Cricket Country* and then draw parallels from it. (Edmund) Blunden was acting in response to human catastrophe. I act only at a point of radical change in the game'.

How deeply ironic those two sentences, written more than 12 months ago, now seem to me.

As I write this, only those blessed with the gift of prophecy can tell you when the cricket season is going to start or when it might end. Counties set off for sunny, far flung corners of the world to practise in March and then came home again before unpacking. Cricket's governing bodies fumbled blindly about like the rest of us, attempting to plan the summer on the basis of guesswork, which is your only option when no one is certain of anything. Players, even the weary who needed a rest, fretted about the length of break that could stretch ahead of them. The financial consequences could be ghastly; especially if Neville Cardus has to rewrite the line about there being no summer in England without cricket.

Coronavirus came in two ways – gradually and then suddenly. There's no need to elaborate on that; you'll all have your own profound stories about it.

I confess that I briefly considered asking the publishers to spike this book. Would anyone care whether it – or any other title – came out or not? Wasn't it all so trivial?

I changed my mind because the events of the past few months underlined a great contradiction. They demonstrated the magnificent triviality of sport in life's great scheme. They also showed how vitally important it is in the weave of so many people's daily lives. When normalcy returns, and we're out in the fresh air again, we'll appreciate and cherish the small pleasures of everyday life even more than we did before. Sport is undoubtedly one of those. It matters too. We can be curmudgeonly about it when it's there, but we miss it terribly when it isn't. Some of us barely know what to do with ourselves. Sport often offers us escapism from the humdrum and also from a lot of the disparate responsibilities and pressures that we'd prefer to dodge or forget.

Also, this book is essentially a celebration of cricket, which is why I wrote it in the first place. It captures not only what I saw, but also what I felt. I hope it reminds you of the thrill and melodrama of the game and some of the beauty within it.

It has long roots.

The calendar tells me that more than a decade has passed since I went travelling hopefully around the country and arrived at what became *A Last English Summer*; which was a book about the 2009 season. That fact, while unarguable, is peculiarly at odds with my memory of the event. I would swear on a stack of *Wisden*s that it happened just a handful of years ago – four or five at most – rather than ten and a half. Here is evidence that age accelerates Time, which rushes on in a great whoosh but does so slyly and subtly; we barely feel the draught as it passes.

Rarely do I re-read my books. The process always makes me think of Thomas Wolfe's dictum: 'You can't go home again'. A book is like a place: never quite as you remember it and hopelessly beyond your grasp to change. But I do recall, very distinctly in fact, stressing one thing about *A Last English Summer* well before it hit the shops. It was this: the older it got, the more relevant it would become.

It's both ridiculous and pretentiously highfalutin to strive, like Enoch Soames, for posterity; you won't be around to see whether your sweat and effort secured so much as a sliver of it. But I thought – and still think – that *A Last English Summer* had half a chance of surviving on the shelves of cricket libraries because it was concerned with the immediate moment. I set off to preserve what I believed would soon perish.

Take a few examples. The book begins in an Antarctic-like chill at Lord's, where I saw the last fixture on 'home' soil that pitted the MCC against the Champion County. It ends in Adelaide-like heat at Canterbury; Kent and Northamptonshire are gently duelling in a competition (the Pro40) that no longer exists. Between that cold early April and that balmy late September, as I toted a notebook and a pencil across our pleasant land, England's Ashes side included Strauss, Pietersen and Flintoff; Australia's included Ponting, Clarke and Johnson.

Doesn't it all seem so close and, paradoxically, so far away?

You may think it strange to summon the ghost of that book here, now and in these circumstances. I do it only to properly explain the source of this one.

I stake no claim for clairvoyance – far from it – but I wrote *A Last English Summer* because I sensed the decisive shift to come from red ball to white. I felt even the senior branch of the service – Test matches – would not be immune. I identified 2009 as a hinge moment in that process.

I explain the motivation behind *One Long and Beautiful Summer* in the opening chapters and so won't repeat myself. Suffice to say, I think of it (as I do *The Kings of Summer*) as a footbridge between what I witnessed in 2009 and what looms ahead for cricket. When the idea originally occurred to me, it seemed merely timely and appropriate. As the summer progressed, it felt a little more urgent and necessary.

Put it this way. I returned home from watching England beat Australia so improbably at Headingley and switched on the TV. West Indies were playing India in the Sir Vivian Richards Stadium. The ground was practically empty. I calculated there were fewer people in the whole place than had occupied the top tier of Yorkshire's Emerald Stand that afternoon. If that isn't alarming, what is?

By a depressing coincidence, the game's administrators are already in a semi-smooch with the prospect of four-day Tests. The cynical among us think we know why a full blown kiss could happen: it'll create space to squeeze in more one-day cricket.

I am grateful to Simon Wilde, estimable cricket correspondent of *The Sunday Times*, for sharpening that point for me. I am unashamedly stealing his homework, published at the end of 2019. Simon wrote: 'Test cricket has not met with the grisly fate many predicted for it – the number of Tests played in 2010–19 is at 433 only slightly lower than the 464 staged from 2000-09 – but it has been overshadowed by the spike from 1,532 to 2,184 ODIs and international Twenty20s played during the same periods.'

I don't know about you, but those figures worry me a tad.

While you contemplate them – probably while heading for the drinks cabinet – I have a little housekeeping to do and a heartfelt thank you to offer to those who contributed in different ways to *One Long and Beautiful Summer*.

I'm very grateful to Paul Smith for sharing his insider information on Menston Cricket Club. I must also pay tribute to two outstanding books by the historian Jack Kell, who wrote about his love for the club and his love for the village.

My primary supporters have been the exceptional Jon Riley

(he also published *A Last English Summer*) and my agent Grainne Fox, as astute as ever. I'm also very grateful to Jasmine Palmer for her work with the proofs and photographs.

The book is dedicated to Peter Wynne-Thomas, the Sage of Trent Bridge. For most of us who write about the game, Peter's advice and counsel is frequently the first we seek out. What we get from him is erudition, immense knowledge, considerable kindness and a cup of tea. I'd go as far as to say that no one outside the publishing world has influenced more cricket titles in ways big and small. I respect him enormously. I like him even more than that.

And finally . . .

For reasons that need not bother us here, I was recently able to pay a public tribute to my wife Mandy at the National Liberal Club. Without her, nothing would get done, let alone written. I made the point – and I wasn't exaggerating – that I couldn't find my socks on my own. Afterwards, a stranger came up to her and introduced himself: 'You must be sock woman,' he said.

I don't know about Mandy, but ever since I've regarded 'sock woman' as a term of endearment in our house.

It seems apt too. We are, after all, a pair; and one of us (guess which one) would be quite useless and serve no purpose without the other.

AUTHOR Q&A

Duncan Hamilton interviewed by Jon Riley

One Long and Beautiful Summer is the third in your 'Summer' series, sitting beside *A Last English Summer* and *The Kings of Summer*. What draws you towards this particular type of book?

A combination of things, really. With a biography, you do your research and then decide what the start, the middle and the end of the book is going to be and also the lines of argument you want to emphasise. You're essentially following a route map of your own creation. With every 'Summer' book I've combined reportage, history, polemic and colour writing. It's a much more demanding thing to do because you don't start with a plot. You're hoping that something will happen – that serendipity will smile on you – because you're very much in the hands of fate. I think of each of those titles as being travel books in the loosest sense of the description. You try to conjure a sense of place and atmosphere and give the reader an idea of why you're there and how you got to a particular spot. I can't remember how old I was when I first read J B Priestley's *English Journey* and Edwin Muir's *Scottish Journey*, but I loved the idea of writing that sort of discursive book. You can go off on tangents. One day – just perhaps – I'll track Priestley's footsteps. He starts off in the 1930s at the quayside at Southampton, where 'a man might first land'. I'd start off at Terminal 5 of Heathrow Airport . . . How times change.

And your use of the word Summer in each title?

There's such a thing as the Proust questionnaire, a parlour game in which every question you answer is supposed to reveal something of your personality. There are several versions of it and one of them asks: What is Your Favourite Word. Mine is Summer – all that mown grass, all those thick hedgerows. I'm not really a winter person. I tend to hibernate between late November and early March.

You say in the acknowledgements that you considered asking me not to publish the book because of Covid-19. What are your thoughts about that now?

At that time we were about to leap into Spring and everything was so surreal that even thinking about cricket seemed a little trivial and preposterously inconsequential. I wasn't convinced the book would be relevant. Who would care about cricket? I'm very relieved now that I didn't ask you not to publish it. The 2019 season became more poignant than ever because we didn't have the 2020 season to enjoy. I think we all clung on to the small pleasures of everyday life simply to get through those months. For some people, such as me, one of those pleasures was thinking about cricket. Every fan I know was reminiscing about where they'd been the previous Summer and also dwelling on what the game meant to them. Our appreciation of cricket grew, rather than diminished, as a consequence.

How did you cope with the loss of the game for so long?

YouTube was helpful. As a way to escape, I could time-travel almost to whichever era suited me. I took refuge in some old books too. Neville Cardus, of course, but also John Arlott, Alan Ross, R C Robertson-Glasgow and David Foot, who is one of my favourite cricket writers because he always caught so well the flavour of the County Championship and the players in it. I tried, but repeatedly got out-bid, to buy *Subbuteo Table Cricke*t on eBay. I had a set when I was a boy and suddenly wished I'd never given it away. In the early days of lockdown even the editions with incomplete or broken figures went for low – or sometimes relatively high – three figure sums. I don't usually dabble in social media, a place where words get weaponised, but I was astonished at the number of cricket fans who posted messages about it and also *Owzat*. Some people went as far as putting the scorecards of their matches on Twitter. You won't believe this, but I'm fairly sure Alastair Cook scored 100,000 runs before the end of April on dining tables across the country. If he ever gets those innings ratified by the Association of Cricket Statisticians, he'll break every record Donald Bradman holds . . .

How well do you think the ECB coped during 2020?

One of the other things I did was keep a scrapbook of the season. It's an A3 hardback, which is actually an artist's sketchbook. I go through it now and I'm still surprised by how much cricket was played in so few weeks. At the beginning, I cut out and pasted in a lot of articles that gave a very gloomy prognosis about the season – especially after Boris Johnson's infamous and fatuous declaration that the ball was a 'vector of disease'. The reader may already know what I think of the ECB's attitude towards the County Championship, but I can't fault the way it put together a package of Test matches and four-day games that I thought we'd never see. They did all that with a lot of dignity too. There was little prevarication, posturing or high and mighty pretention. English Premier League football ought to have learnt from them. I think cricket – and cricketers – generally came out of the summer with considerable credit.

Do you think perceptions of cricket changed during 2020?

Wisden asked me to write a piece for the 2021 Almanack that is essentially based around that very question. The short answer is yes. The longer answer, which you'll find in what I wrote for them, is that even people who wouldn't regard themselves as dedicated fans missed the game to one degree or another after realising how integral it is to our summers. I lost count of the number of times I read the Cardus quote: 'There can be no summer in this land without cricket'. But 2020 proved he was right. The newspapers published a hefty stack of photographs of lovely county, town and village grounds that were there to show us how lovely a match can look. They were there to remind us about how much cricket is part of the landscape between April and September. That hoary, clichéd line about not missing something until it's gone happens to be true. We grew to love cricket even more through its absence. We measured the size of the hole it left, not only at the professional level, but also at the grass roots. Perhaps we won't take it for granted again.

Did anything else help cricket's standing and increase public awareness?

Two things, I'm certain. The first is the way that the game conducted itself. There were lots of stories – far too many to mention – about the good deeds cricketers did on behalf of the community and in particularly for the NHS. Think of Jos Buttler, who auctioned the shirt he wore in the World Cup final and raised more than £65,000. Think of others who took food parcels to people's homes or shopped for those unable to go further than their front doorstep. The second is the streaming service which enabled first members, and then everyone else, to watch the Championship from their tablet or laptop or TV. When it began, I was on holiday in Worcester-shire. I was watching Notts v Yorkshire at Trent Bridge while Lancashire, who'd been displaced from Old Trafford by the Test series, were facing Leicestershire at New Road, which was only a 45-minute drive away from the house I'd rented. Like most of what happened last summer, that seemed quite bizarre to me. As the season progressed, I could hop effort-lessly from Canterbury to Arundel and from Headingley to anywhere. Streaming opened up the whole of the county game to anyone who wanted to drop in and watch it.

Did you also enjoy watching cricket on the BBC again?

As much as I'd never willingly part with my Sky subscription – the analysis, commentary and innovative production are gold star standard – I think Test cricket needs to be on the BBC regularly in some shape or form. There's a cachet about being connected with the corporation that other terrestrial broadcasters can't match. Firstly, it's about history. Secondly, it's about the promotional reach of the BBC. I confess that I watched the programmes with sound turned down, but that's only because I don't like artificial crowd noise. It was like having your head pushed into a beehive.

You're especially devoted to the County Championship and to red-ball cricket in general. Do you think what happened in 2020 has put the competition in more or less danger in the future?

Sadly, I think it's going to be far tougher for the Championship to survive in its present form over the coming seasons. I'd be delighted, but also astonished, if we still had eighteen full time, first class counties ten years from now. I think the creation of the Bob Willis Trophy showed us the road down which the ECB would prefer to travel. That means small groups – perhaps of only five or six teams in two divisions – and counties playing either ten or twelve four day matches each summer. You'll also find, I fear, that the Championship will always bookend the season, leaving the middle of it for the white-ball competitions.

Are still so strongly opposed to The Hundred?

Absolutely. The ECB's whole strategy is based on making this competition a success - irrespective of the damage created elsewhere. There's no doubt that some people, especially those who don't watch cricket at the moment, will be attracted to The Hundred. But will there be enough of them? And where does that leave those of us who don't want another white-ball competition in the first place? I'm concerned about how long the novelty of The Hundred will last. In the whirlpool of the world – where fads and fashions alter so quickly – nothing is 'modern' for very long. Twenty20 is proof of that. The Hundred is an enormous spin of the roulette wheel for the ECB. It would be a big bet to lose, the equivalent of no longer having a roof over your head. But I do hope I'm wrong about it.

When cricket returns, where are the places that you most want to go?

One of the most evocative pieces Neville Cardus ever wrote tells of his return to Britain from Australia after the Second World War. He saw everything afresh and mostly with a sense of wonder. I imagine that's the way I'll feel when I step inside a ground again. I got a little advance notice of the fixtures. Within two minutes of looking at them – and I'm not exaggerating – I booked my hotel for the Roses Match at Scarborough in case someone else beat me to it. In my mind, I'm already strolling through the gate on North Marine Road after walking along the coastal path that overlooks the North Sea. I'll also go to Trent Bridge as soon as it's possible to get there.

You've written a biography of Cardus, how would he have made it through the barren months?

He was a man who could just about boil a kettle. He also wrote with a fountain pen and, like me, never learned how to drive a car. I doubt he'd have been on Zoom. It would have been especially difficult for him because so much of his social life was attached to his work. He lived for most of his adult life in the National Liberal Club. I like to think he'd have got some company there when he needed it. I also like to think he'd have written a book during lockdown. Perhaps, it would have been the biography he ought to have done, which was the life of his boyhood hero Reggie Spooner.

What kind of response did you receive from readers after *One Long and Beautiful Summer* came out?

I'll say firstly that I was amazed the book was one of the catalysts for a leader in the *Guardian* and got a mention in the *New Yorker*, a magazine not exactly known for its coverage of the County Championship. Above all, though, the most satisfying thing was the reaction of readers. When I write a book, I never imagine anyone reading it. Anyone who picks up *One Long and Beautiful Summer* will discover which village I live in. It's near the foot of the Yorkshire Dales. I began to get letters that contained nothing on the envelope but my name, my profession and the name of the village. Every writer articulated his or her own memories of the game and their trepidation about The Hundred. Reading them confirmed that I wasn't alone in my opinions and also how much cricket means to so many people. I hope we protect it.

Jon Riley, publisher of Riverrun, commissioned and edited One Long and Beautiful Summer *as well as Duncan Hamilton's* A Last English Summer *and* Harold Larwood.

List of Images

Select Bibliography

Books

Arlott, J., *Vintage Summer: 1947*, Eyre and Spottiswoode, 1967

How to Watch Cricket, Unwin, 1949 (and later editions)

Anderson, D., *Echoes From A Golden Age*, Boundary Books, 2010

Blunden, E., *Cricket Country*, Collins, 1944

The Face of England, Longmans, 1933

Undertones of War, Cobden-Sanderson, 1928

Cooper, Z. and Lightman, D., *Cricket Grounds from the Air*, Myriad, 2010

Crowe, M., *Out on a Limb*, Reed 1995

Doshi, A., *Tendulkar in Wisden*, John Wisden, 2016

Edwards, A., *Regency Buck*, Robson, 2001

Elborough, T. and Rennison, N., *A London Year*, Frances Lincoln, 2013

Frith, D., *Frith's Encounters*, VKP, 2014

Gordon, H., *Sussex County Cricket*, Convoy Publications, 1950

Heald, T., *The Character of Cricket*, Pavilion, 1986

Jenkinson, N., *Cricket's Greatest Comeback*, J. W. McKenzie, 1998

Johnston, B. and Webber, R. (ed.), *Armchair Cricket*, BBC, 1957

Johnston, B. (ed.), *Armchair Cricket*, BBC, 1975

Keating, F., *Half-Time Whistle*, Robson, 1992

Kelner, M., *Sit Down and Cheer: A History of Sport on TV*, Bloomsbury, 2012

Lee, C., *From The Sea End, The Official History of Sussex County Cricket Club*, Partridge Press, 1989

Marshall, M., *Gentlemen and Players, Conversations with Cricketers*, Grafton, 1987

Mee, A., *The King's England: Somerset*, Hodder, 1941

Meyer, M., *Summer Days, Writers on Cricket*, Eyre Methuen, 1981

Page, R., *The Decline of an English Village*, Quiller, 2019

Parker, E., *Between the Wickets*, Philip Allan, 1926

Plumptre, G., *Homes of Cricket*, Queen Anne Press, 1988

Pridham, C. H. B., *The Charm of Cricket Past and Present*, Herbert Jenkins, 1949

Priestley, J. B., *Delight*, Readers' Union Edition, 1951

Prittie, T. C. F., *Cricket North and South*, SBC edition, 1955

Roberts, R. A., *The Cricketer's Bedside Book*, Batsford, 1966

Robertson-Glasgow, R. C., *46 Not Out*, Hollis and Carter, 1948

Sampson, A., *Grounds of Appeal: The Homes of First-Class Cricket*, Robert Hale, 1981

Stapleton, L., *A Sussex Cricket Odyssey*, Ian Harrap, 1979

Tendulkar, S., *Playing It My Way*, Hodder, 2014

Rothkopf, C. Z., *Selected Letters of Siegfried Sassoon and Edmund Blunden, 1919–1967* (three volumes), Pickering and Chatto, 2012

Wilde, S., *Ranji: A Genius Rich and Strange*, The Kingswood Press, 1990

Webb, B., *Edmund Blunden, A Biography*, Yale, 2000

Yardley, N. W. D. and Kilburn, J. M., *Homes of Sport: Cricket*, Peter Garnett Ltd, 1952
A Country Vicar, *The Happy Cricketer*, Frederick Muller, 1946
Wisden: Various Editions
The Cricketers' Who's Who, various editions

No author

A Century of Bradford League Cricket, 1903–2003 (published by the League)
M.C.C., 1787–1937, The Times, 1937
Sachin Tendulkar: The Man Cricket Loved Back, Penguin India, 2014

Newspapers and magazines

Country Life, 26 May 1944
ESPNcricinfo, 5 April 2009
The *Guardian*, 22 January 1974; 11 June 1988
Illustrated London News, 10 June 1944
The *Listener*, 26 September 1946
Manchester Evening News, 20 April 1944
The *Observer*, 7 May 1944
The *Scribe*, 28 June 1944
The Sunday Times, 17 June 1962
The Times, 3 May 1985
Times Literary Supplement, 29 April 1944; 4 June 1952

Index